The

Labrador
Retriever

An Owner's Guide To

A HAPPY HEALTHY PET

Howell Book House

Howell Book House
A Simon & Schuster Macmillan Company
1633 Broadway
New York, NY 10019

MACMILLAN is a registered trademark of Macmillan, Inc.

Library of Congress Cataloging-in-Publication Data

Weiss-Agresta, Lisa.
    The Labrador retriever : an owner's guide to a happy, healthy pet / by Lisa Weiss-Agresta.
        p. cm.
    Includes bibliographical references
    ISBN 0-87605-378-9
    1. Labrador retriever.   I. Title.
SF429.L3W45   1995
636.7'52—dc20   95-24281
    CIP

Manufactured in the United States of America
10 9 8 7 6 5 4 3 2 1

Series Director: Dominique De Vito
Series Assistant Director: Felice Primeau
Book Design: Michele Laseau
Cover Design: Iris Jeromnimon
Illustration: Jeff Yesh
Photography:
    Cover: adult: Paulette Braun, Pets by Paulette; puppy: Mollie Weiss
    Courtesy of the American Kennel Club: 14, 16, 22
    Joan Balzarini: 96
    Mary Bloom: 26, 59, 72, 76, 96, 136, 145
    Paulette Braun/Pets by Paulette: 7, 20, 38, 96
    Buckinghamhill American Cocker Spaniels: 148
    Sian Cox: 134
    Dr. Ian Dunbar: 98, 101, 103, 111, 116–117, 122, 123, 127
    Dan Lyons: 43, 96
    Cathy Merrithew: 129
    Liz Palika: 133
    Janice Raines: 65, 86, 132
    Susan Rezy: 96–97
    Judith Strom: 27, 30, 31, 41, 47, 96, 107, 110, 128, 130, 135, 137, 139, 140, 144, 149, 150
    Mollie Weiss: i, 25, 36, 42, 45, 48, 52, 54, 58, 61
    Kerrin Winter / Dale Churchill: 2–3, 5, 8, 9, 10, 12, 13, 18, 23, 34–35, 55, 56, 62
Production Team: Troy Barnes, John Carroll, Jama Carter, Kathleen Caulfield, Trudy Coler, Vic Peterson, Terri Sheehan, Marvin Van Tiem, Amy DeAngelis and Kathy Iwasaki

Contents

Welcome
to the
World
of the

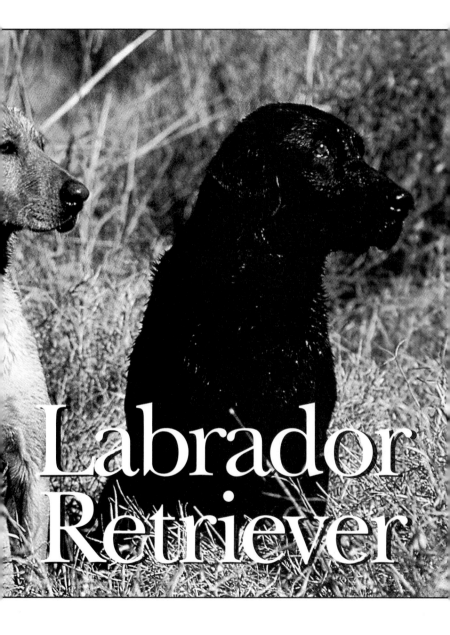

part one

Labrador Retriever

External Features of the Labrador Retriever

What
is a
Labrador
Retriever?

A Labrador puppy is a bouncy bundle of black, yellow or chocolate fun and energy. A Labrador adult is one of many things. Versatility is its middle name. A Lab might be your guide dog if you are sightless or visually impaired: The Labrador Retriever is the breed used most often as guide dogs for the blind. Because they love to fetch for their masters, Labs are very popular as service dogs for those who are wheelchair bound. If you work with detector dogs, the Labrador is probably your breed of choice because of its keen nose. The Labrador is the best breed

for detecting drugs, explosives and arson. If hunting is your sport, you know that Labs are the most popular hunting companions of all the retrieving breeds. Eager-to-please Labs make great Therapy dogs, bringing joy to people confined to hospitals and nursing homes.

Should you decide to become involved with showing for conformation or competing in obedience or field trials, once again, Labs are very popular for all three competitions. When it's time for your family to choose a pet, you probably can't go wrong with a Labrador if you are an active family on the go and want a dog who will be on the go, too. Because of their happy-go-lucky attitude, Labs are great with children and adults. A Lab is never happier than when he's with his family or his person.

Now, I may be prejudiced when I say that the Labrador is one of the most wonderful and amazing breeds ever developed. Over the last thirty years, my family and I have had the good fortune to share our homes with some very special four-legged creatures, each a true Labrador, but each with its own unique personality, likes and dislikes. Many of them were very funny characters who enjoyed entertaining us endlessly.

General Description

What constitutes a "good" Labrador is outlined in the breed's official American Kennel Club (AKC) standard. Every breed has a standard that is a comprehensive list of the specific characteristics that make one breed distinct from another. You can obtain a copy of any breed's standard from the AKC. After reading a breed's standard, you should be able to visualize a well-balanced specimen of that breed. A picture, along with the narrative of a dog considered to be a very good specimen, is usually included. There really is no perfect dog: Breeders are always striving to breed dogs that come as close to the standard as possible, but when you're dealing with living creatures, the variables are numerous.

WHAT IS A BREED STANDARD?

A breed standard—a detailed description of an individual breed—is meant to portray the *ideal* specimen of that breed. This includes ideal structure, temperament, gait, type—all aspects of the dog. Because the standard describes an ideal specimen, it isn't based on any particular dog. It is a concept against which judges compare actual dogs and breeders strive to produce dogs. At a dog show, the dog that wins is the one that comes closest, in the judge's opinion, to the standard for its breed. Breed standards are written by the breed parent clubs, the national organizations formed to oversee the well-being of the breed. They are voted on and approved by the members of the parent clubs.

The Labrador Retriever standard was changed recently. The old as well as the new standard says the Labrador should be a medium-sized dog. To me that may mean twenty inches; to you, medium may mean twenty-five inches—different strokes for different folks. I think Labs should fall into the "bigger than a Springer Spaniel and smaller than a Newfoundland" category. Balance, structure, temperament and working ability should all be considered more important than size. I don't believe that an otherwise good, well-balanced Labrador can be the wrong size! This dog is now so versatile that there are needs and uses for Labradors of all sizes. Though temperament is not a physical trait, it is a hallmark of this breed. The Labrador's kindly temperament is visible in its warm eyes as well as in its body language.

A favorable Lab will have a distinct head.

The Labrador should be a medium-sized dog, giving the appearance of a dog that is strong, muscular and active. The head, which includes a very specific kind and friendly expression, the coat and the tail are, in my opinion, this breed's three outstanding characteristics. The head, coat, tail and temperament, all worn on the correct body or frame, are what give you the complete Labrador. If any of these things is missing, you don't have a Labrador. It's a package deal.

The Head

Let's start at the head and work our way to the toes. As I said, the head is one of the breed's most distinguishing characteristics. It should not remind you of any other breed. If it reminds you of a Coonhound, a Great Dane or some kind of Terrier, then it's not a correct Labrador head. The Lab has a fairly broad back skull and a nice stop. The stop connects the skull to the muzzle, and the eyes are set into the stop. The skull and muzzle run on practically parallel planes. The head should not have big, heavy, apple cheeks or flews that are too pendulous. The head should have a neat, clean appearance unlike the sloppy or drooling look that is appropriate for a Saint Bernard. The muzzle should be strong and never snipey looking. The nose should be wide with well-developed nostrils, for that keen olfactory sense. A Labrador should have what is called a "scissors bite," where the top front teeth come down right over (actually touching) the bottom front teeth, just as the blades of a pair of scissors cross each other to cut something. A level bite, where the top and bottom meet at exactly the same place, is acceptable but not desirable. Labradors should have full dentition and should not be overshot or undershot, where there is a gap of one-eighth to one-quarter inch or more between the top and bottom jaw. Either of these conditions or a wry mouth (crooked jaw) would make it harder for the dog to carry game. If your dog is a family pet, it probably will not matter if his bite is not perfect. He will probably never miss a meal.

Good ears add to the complete feel of the head.

Ears: The ears should be set off the side of the skull, not too high and not too low. They should be of medium size, hanging so that the bottom tips are about two inches below the eyes. The ears should not be so big or so small that they draw attention to themselves. And they should never be long or folded as they are on many hounds.

Eyes: The Labrador's eyes are where we see that irresistible, sweet, kind and alert expression. I like the shape of the eye to be like a rounded diamond. Although some round eyes can be attractive, they should not resemble the round eyes of a Cocker Spaniel, nor should they be too almond-shaped. I prefer a warm brown eye on all three colors (black, yellow or chocolate), maybe a bit darker on a yellow Lab. If the eyes are too light, the dog's expression will be ruined. There should never be a harsh or mean look about a Labrador. When you look into a Lab's eyes, you should feel instant friendliness. Usually, the moment your eyes meet, the Lab's powerful tail starts wagging automatically and that's it—you're buddies!

The Body

Neck: The desirable Labrador head should sit on a strong neck of medium length. If the neck is too short, the dog looks as if its head is sitting on its shoulders; if the neck is too long, the dog appears elegant, like a setter, which is not correct. There is nothing elegant about this dog. He should remind you of a little Mack truck—agile, but strong and sturdy.

As you continue down the neck, past the withers, the top line (the back) should be rather level, never swayback or sloping to the degree that a Setter's back does from the neck to the rump.

The chest should be deep with well-sprung ribs like a barrel. The shoulders should be long and sloping. The correct look requires long bones that form a ninety-degree angle as you look at the dog from the side, from the withers, to the sternum, to the elbow. The front legs are well underneath the dog, allowing a prominent breastbone to show and creating the picture of a powerful chest.

Three fine examples of Labrador Retrievers

Legs: All four legs should have good, thick bone, the front legs coming straight down from the shoulders. The rear legs should be well bent at the knee or stifle. The hind quarters should be thick with well-muscled thighs. The hocks should not be too long and should also be well bent and well let down (not one continuous line from buttocks to the foot). Picture about a six-inch section from the foot to the hock joint and then a little jog, toward the front, and on up to the stifle. The view from behind the dog should not be narrow but rather hefty with "good buns!"

Tail: The tail should be set right off the back. In other words, you should see one straight line from the withers to the tip of the tail. If the croup drops off too steeply and the tail is set too low or if the tail is set too high, the picture will be spoiled.

Even resting, these Labs look eager.

As a Labrador moves, the tail usually wags happily from side to side. It should never be carried curled up over the back like a hound's tail. A tail that is carried too low or between the legs will give the appearance of timidity. *Timidity* is a word that is not in the Labrador dictionary. This very important tail, which should not be too long (not below the hock), acts like a rudder when the dog is swimming. We call it an otter tail because it's thick at the base and tapers down to a tip, like the tail of an otter. The tail should be well covered with a very distinctive short, dense coat. The underside of the tail should never have any long feathery hair on it.

Coat

All three colors of the Labrador are solid colors: black, yellow or chocolate. A white spot on the chest is permissible. All the colors should have the correct double coat. The thick undercoat lies under the topcoat. The topcoat should be a bit rough to the touch and doesn't have to lie flat. In fact, if the coat is too slick, the dog probably doesn't have a good undercoat and would not be useful as a retriever in cold waters. The undercoat acts as insulation and, working in conjunction with the coat's natural oil, helps to repel water. Therefore, the Labrador doesn't feel the cold the way a single-coated dog does. Another aspect of this coat is the special look that it gives the Labrador. As my friend and fellow breeder Kendall Herr says, "The Labrador has a unique stuffed-animal look, which is obtained by the double coat with a thick undercoat that fills in and rounds out any angular look." The coat makes him look like a big, eighty-five-pound teddy bear.

The Whole Picture

It's most important for the Labrador to be well balanced. He should not be as tall and thin as a pointer, and he should not be as short and fat as a potbellied pig. No one feature should be so prominent as to detract from the total picture. If you look at a Labrador and notice only its huge head, the dog is probably unbalanced. If you look at a Labrador and see only its big feet or a long scraggly tail, you're probably not looking at a good specimen of the breed.

Serious breeders try very hard to take the total Labrador into consideration when thinking about breeding a litter. In choosing the right male for your female, the proper health clearances are, of course, important, but they are just the tip of the iceberg. A breeder must know

> ## THE AMERICAN KENNEL CLUB
>
> Familiarly referred to as "the AKC," the American Kennel Club is a nonprofit organization devoted to the advancement of purebred dogs. The AKC maintains a registry of recognized breeds and adopts and enforces rules for dog events including shows, obedience trials, field trials, hunting tests, lure coursing, herding, earthdog trials, agility and the Canine Good Citizen program. It is a club of clubs, established in 1884 and composed, today, of over 500 autonomous dog clubs throughout the United States. Each club is represented by a delegate; the delegates make up the legislative body of the AKC, voting on rules and electing directors. The American Kennel Club maintains the Stud Book, the record of every dog ever registered with the AKC, and publishes a variety of materials on purebred dogs, including a monthly magazine, books and numerous educational pamphlets. For more information, contact the AKC at the address listed in Chapter 13, "Resources," and look for the names of their publications in Chapter 12, "Recommended Reading."

that both dogs are of sound body and mind. They must have that proper double coat, that kind expression and that otter tail, along with that wonderful, eager-to-please personality.

Breeding is a lot like baking: If you don't have the proper ingredients, in the proper proportions, the

product won't be right. You don't make cookies without sugar. You don't make chocolate cake without eggs. Many key ingredients in baking are important to the product but may not be the outwardly obvious ingredients as, for example, the chocolate in the chocolate cake. Just try making a cake without eggs. It has been done, but the product is lacking. Try to breed Labradors without all the right ingredients, and you will surely have a flop on your hands.

A good Labrador will want to please and, therefore, will be easy to train for obedience. He will possess a keen sense of smell and an athletic body. All these quali-

A face anyone could love.

ties make the Labrador the perfect hunting companion. Whether black, yellow or chocolate, the dog has a distinct look, singular to the Lab.

The Labrador Retriever's Ancestry

There are many theories about the origin of the breed known today as the Labrador Retriever. One point on which all historians seem to agree is that the Labrador originally came from Newfoundland, not Labrador. They were known by several names like the St. John's Water Dog, the Little Newfoundlander and the Black Water Dog, before officially being dubbed the Labrador Retriever.

Many books have been written about the origin of this wonderful breed. However, if a half-dozen old-time breeders gather in a room, a hot debate on the dog's origin is sure to ensue. James Dickie wrote in his book *The Dog* (Philadelphia: J. P. Lippincott, circa 1935, p. 130), "There are a few people alive who must know the whole story—how interesting it would be if they would write it."

Some believe that the Labrador was developed by the fishermen off the coast of Newfoundland and that it was the result of an attempt to scale down the Newfoundland dog. In other words, they wanted to produce a somewhat smaller dog because the Newfies were a bit cumbersome. The dog had to be a good retriever. He also had to have good bone and strong limbs to pull heavy loads. He needed a dense coat thick enough to withstand the cold water, but one that would not ball up with ice. He had to be eager to please, able to swim great distances and happy to live on a diet of fish and whatever else could be scrounged up. The Labrador became that dog. But how? That is the mystery. Some believe that the large Newfoundland dogs were indigenous to Newfoundland; others believe there were no dogs there until the Europeans came to the coast to fish.

The Newfoundland is a wonderful breed. My family had three of them along with our many Labradors when I was a child, and it's easy for me to see some of the similarities between the breeds. In many ways, Newfoundlands are like Labradors in big bear suits. Unfortunately, like many other giant breeds, some inherent problems plaguing the breed at times make owning them heartbreaking, though they are very sweet and gentle.

"Dual Ch. Bracken's Sweep" winner of the 7th Annual National Championship Retriever Trial in 1947.

In trying to decide which theory to relate, I spoke with many friends who are longtime breeders. I'm quite lucky to have grown up on Long Island, where Labradors really got their foothold in this country. Many, if not most, early English imports came to Long Island. I'm also lucky to have Mrs. Curtis Read as a friend.

Mrs. Read

Mrs. Read, the former Joan Redmond, got her first Labrador in 1930. Her dog, Champion Bancstone Bob of Wingan, came from Jay Carlisle's Wingan Kennels and was sired by the famous English import, Dual Champion Bramshaw Bob, out of Drinkstone Peg. From a litter of seven, five became champions. Mrs. Read is still breeding Labs under the Chidley prefix as well as breeding Norfolk and Norwich Terriers. In 1933, she became the first Junior Member of the Labrador Retriever Club of America. That same year, she exhibited her dog at the first show of the Labrador Retriever Club of America. The show was held in New York City on 74th Street in a garage owned by Marshall Field. Mrs. Read's home is both a library and a museum for the breed, and she is the curator. Over the last thirty years, Mrs. Read has graciously allowed me to spend countless hours there, looking through books, pictures and Labrador stuff! Mrs. Read invited my father, sister and me to attend and exhibit at the Long Island Kennel Club's 1966 match, held at the Platt's estate, and there we were bitten by the "dog show bug."

Mrs. Read let me borrow *The Labrador Dog* by Franklin B. Lord (published privately, Labrador Retriever Club, 1945). Lord's book starts with an extract from *A History of the Skuykill Fishing Company*, which according to him was at that

WHERE DID DOGS COME FROM?

It can be argued that dogs were right there at man's side from the beginning of time. As soon as human beings began to document their existence, the dog was among their drawings and inscriptions. Dogs were not just friends, they served a purpose: There were dogs to hunt birds, pull sleds, herd sheep, burrow after rats—even sit in laps! What your dog was originally bred to do influences the way it behaves. The American Kennel Club recognizes over 140 breeds, and there are hundreds more distinct breeds around the world. To make sense of the breeds, they are grouped according to their size or function. The AKC has seven groups:

1) Sporting, 2) Working,
3) Herding, 4) Hounds,
5) Terriers, 6) Toys,
7) Nonsporting

Can you name a breed from each group? Here's some help: (1) Golden Retriever; (2) Doberman Pinscher; (3) Collie; (4) Beagle; (5) Scottish Terrier; (6) Maltese; and (7) Dalmatian. All modern domestic dogs (*Canis familiaris*) are related, however different they look, and are all descended from *Canis lupus*, the gray wolf.

time (1945) "the oldest club in the world." He thought the following to be a fitting description of a Labrador: "If you look to its antiquity, it is most ancient. If to its dignity, it is most honorable" (p. 12). Lord continues, "Those who really want to get a thorough knowledge of the Labrador dog and its history should study 'The Labrador Dog, Its Home and History' by Lord George Scott and Sir John Middleton, London, 1936 . . ." (p. 12).

Scott is quoted in Lord's book as saying,

> It appears that the aboriginal inhabitants of the island, the Beothucks, did not have any dogs. The English began to fish in Newfoundland in 1498; the Portuguese came in 1501; and the French in 1504. The English were the only fishermen who engaged in shore fishery and made certain settlements about 1522. Most of the settlers came from Devon and were hunters. They wanted dogs for hunting and to retrieve their fish so they probably took the dogs that were then common in England over with them. There are references to a grey hound and a mastiff on the island as far back as 1611. These dogs brought by the men of Devon were the only canine population of Newfoundland and were bred and trained to meet the needs of their owners. From these various breeds of dogs bred over a period of 280 years under rigorous conditions there were evolved the Newfoundland dog and the Labrador. They were the product of the environment and survival and perhaps selection. (p. 14)

Ch. Bancory Trump of Wingan, 1934.

Scott and Middleton offer the following:

> The Labrador dog did not come from Labrador but from Newfoundland, mostly from the vicinity

of St. James and White Bay. There were two kinds of dogs on Newfoundland, the big, long-haired, black dog known as the Newfoundland, and the small short-haired dog known as the Labrador of St. John's breed. (p. 12)

Scott quotes Colonel Hawker from his book *Advice to Young Sportsmen* (London, 1814) as he describes the two breeds:

> Here we are a little in the dark. Every canine brute that is nearly as big as a jackass and as hairy as a bear, is denominated a fine Newfoundland dog. Very different, however, . . . are the St. Johns breed of these animals. (p. 12)

> The other (the Labrador), by far the best for every kind of shooting, is oftener black than any other color . . . pretty deep in chest; . . . has short or smooth hair; does not carry his tail so much curled as the other; and is extremely quick and active in running, swimming. (p. 12)

> Their sense of smelling is scarcely to be credited. Their discrimination of scent, in following a wounded pheasant through a whole covert full of game, or pinioned wild fowl through a furze brake or warren of rabbits, appears almost impossible. (p. 12)

Lord further tells us that

> The dogs were used by the fishermen . . . to haul in the winter's wood and to retrieve fish that had become unhooked. It seems that the fish which were taken at great depth often became unhooked near the surface and the dogs were sent overboard to retrieve them. (p. 13)

No one seems to know exactly when the first of these dogs arrived in England. Lord says that Lord George Scott and Leslie Sprake, authors of *The Labrador Retriever* (London, 1933), agree that

. . . it was the last decade of the 18th century or the first decade of the 19th . . . Shooting Journals of the Second Earl of Malmesbury (1778–1841) which proves that he had what he called a Newfoundland dog in December 1809. Scott seems to think that these were the small dogs that Peter Hawker described at about the same period. (p. 13)

A true retriever.

Lord also tells us that there is further evidence to support these facts because the "Third Earl of Malmesbury (1807–1889) who inherited the kennel is quoted as saying 'we always called mine Labrador dogs and I have kept the breed as pure as I could from the first I had from Poole'" (p. 13).

Most historians of the breed agree that the run between Newfoundland and Poole Harbour, in Dorset, was a common one. The fishermen went back and forth to sell their salted codfish. The dogs often made the trip as well. Sometime around 1818, some of these dogs were seen and purchased. The English waterfowlers were quick to appreciate these talented dogs. The Second Earl of Malmesbury was said to have purchased several from some of the boats' captains. The Third Earl of Malmesbury continued to import and breed the dogs. Although the earl said that he kept his as pure as possible, it's likely that at some point the dogs were bred with the retrievers that were being used before the fishermen arrived (to improve the local dogs). Some believe that Colonel Hawker was the first to write about the dogs and that he was actually the one to dub them Labradors; others disagree.

The Third Earl of Malmesbury gave some of his dogs to the Sixth Earl of Buccleigh, and it was he who actually started keeping good breeding records. Some of our American Labs can be traced to these dogs.

In 1904, The Kennel Club (England) listed Labradors as a separate breed. Before that time, "Retriever" covered the broad category of all retrievers. Labs were gaining popularity by leaps and bounds, winning at field trials and in the ring at dog shows. In 1932 and 1933, the famous Dual Champion (Ch.) Bramshaw Bob was Best-in-Show at Crufts. Crufts is the English equivalent of our Westminster, even though Westminster is a somewhat smaller show. Dual Ch. Bramshaw Bob was owned by the Banchory Kennel, one of the breed's most famous kennels. This kennel belonged to the late Lorna Countess Howe, remembered for doing so much to promote this breed.

Thanks to some who liked the yellow color and made great efforts to strengthen it, we now know and enjoy yellow Labs. The late Mrs. Arthur Wormald (Veronica), of the Knaith Kennels, was one. She started the Yellow Labrador Retriever Club. Some years later, chocolates became more readily accepted as "true" Labradors.

The Labrador Retriever in the United States

Labradors were being imported to the United States and were popular before World War I. Though the AKC grouped them together with the other retrievers, those who were active in sport shooting considered the Labrador Retrievers the best. Many serious breeders from Long Island not only imported the dogs, but also expert kennel men and gamekeepers from Europe.

By the latter part of the 1920s, the AKC recognized the Labrador Retriever as a separate breed. The Labrador Club of America was founded on Long Island late in 1930, and Mrs. Marshall Field became the first president from 1931 to 1935. Mr. Franklin B. Lord and Mr. Robert Goelet were co–vice presidents. Mrs. Marshall Field judged the first specialty show in 1933, as I mentioned earlier, in a garage in New York City. There were thirty-four entries, and the winner was Boli of Blake, owned by Mr. Lord.

In the 1920s and 1930s, when most Labradors were dual-purpose dogs and being run in trials as well as competing at bench events, many famous Long Island families were involved in these competitions. Some of the famous included the Phipps, the Marshall Fields, J. P. Morgan (Mrs. Read told me Morgan had an import called Bancory Snow, who would bring him his slippers and may also have been the first yellow import), Wilton Lloyd Smith and the Whitneys.

The Lab Today

Today, at our Labrador Specialty Shows, it's not unusual to have an entry of 700 or more dogs. The Labrador Retriever Club of the Potomac in Leesburg, Virginia; The Miami Valley Labrador Retriever Club in Middletown, Ohio; and The Mid-Jersey Labrador Retriever Club, Heightstown, New Jersey, are probably the three biggest Lab shows in the country.

Today's Labrador show community is trying to bring about dual-, triple- and multipurpose Labradors. Club members and breeders are encouraged to strive to breed Labradors that look like Labradors, hunt like Labradors and can do tracking tests, obedience trials and search and rescue work, be working companions for the handicapped, eyes for the blind and partners for police detectives involved with narcotics, arson and explosives. A well-bred Labrador can do it all! Fetching dead birds is only the beginning of what this dog can do.

Awaiting her command.

Hard Workers: Today, the U.S. Bureau of Alcohol, Tobacco and Firearms uses Labradors almost exclusively as explosive- and arson-sniffing dogs. They find the Lab's nose to be unrivaled by that of any other breed. And again, a Lab's willingness to please makes the dog a pleasure to work with.

Most police forces employ Labs as their drug and arson detector dogs. Most of the dogs live with the officers to whom they are assigned. Labs easily switch gears from family dogs to dependable partners in fighting crime. Their keen noses, determination and desire to please their masters have earned them the respect that was once reserved for German Shepherds.

If hunting is your passion, again look no further: you have found the dog you need. Many a hunter has told me that because their noses are so keen and because they are so versatile, Labs make the best hunting companions. Their willingness to enter and reenter the water, no matter how cold, puts them at the head of the line in front of all other retrievers.

If you like competition and enjoy dog shows, Labs are great. They require very little grooming and should be shown in their natural state, unlike many other breeds that require hours of grooming and coat care daily or before going into the show ring. In the show ring they are usually very jovial hams!

If you like obedience competition, you won't be alone if the Labrador is your choice. No matter where you live you probably won't have to go far to find an obedience class to learn the basics. When you decide to compete, you'll find plenty of shows that offer obedience classes in every state. Whether or not you plan to go into competition, your Labrador should have basic obedience training. You and your Labrador will both be happier for the experience.

Labradors are now the number-one breed used as guide dogs in the United States as well as in other countries. Because they are easy to groom, are so willing to please and are not easy to intimidate, Labs are perfect for this job. There are over a dozen guide dog schools in this country. I have been associated with The Guide Dog Foundation in Smithtown, New York, for many years. It's one of the oldest schools in the country.

**FAMOUS
OWNERS OF
LABRADOR
RETRIEVERS**

Chuck Barris

Gary
Cooper

Henry
Kissinger

Joan Lundon

Barbara
Mandrell

Kevin
McReynolds

Queen
Elizabeth

Robert
Redford

Mortimer
Zuckerman

Labradors are still very popular in the United Kingdom. In England, you seem to see them everywhere. They are on the streets, in yards, in Hyde Park and even in restaurants. Their popularity is probably due in part to the fact that the Queen of England keeps and breeds Labradors under the prefix Sandringham, as did her father, King George V.

Friends, 1969.

Today we are seeing more and more Labradors winning in the ring, competing in the obedience ring and racking up titles at the AKC Hunting Retriever Tests (different from Field Trials—they test the dog's true hunting ability). There are quite a few champions with Junior and Senior Hunter titles. Ch. Dickendall Ruffy, Sr. Hunter, owned by Kendall Herr of Gainesville, Texas, is a Specialty Show winner, a top producer and a superb hunter. There are others, and, I hope, many more to come.

The **World**

According to the
Labrador
Retriever

If Labs could place personal ads in newspapers looking for their owners, the ad might read something like this:

> *NYLP (nice yellow lab pup) seeks owner with lots of free time who loves to hike, swim, run and play!*

Is a Lab for You?

If you get a Lab and you don't really have the time to spend with it, you will probably have problems. If you lead a sedentary life and you've already bought a Lab—change your lifestyle! If you lead a sedentary life and haven't chosen a dog yet—get a Bulldog!

While they have numerous wonderful qualities, the Labrador Retriever is not the right breed for everyone. There are breeds that

23

come into a home and seem to be happy exploring outside alone and thrive on little attention from the people in the house. These breeds are sweet and loving but fairly independent. Not Labradors! They really need to go to homes where working with and caring for the dog is looked upon as fun, not a chore. Their appetite for attention is almost insatiable. If you want a dog that's going to be happy sleeping in the sun on a nice fluffy pillow, you'll be disappointed in your Lab.

The Labrador Retriever is not, as it's often called, "the perfect pet." I hear people say, "Labs are great: they're low maintenance." I don't believe this is true. The Labrador Retriever may not be the right dog for every family with two kids, a minivan and a fenced-in yard. Labs may be low maintenance from the standpoint of grooming: their coats will almost take care of themselves. Also, they are generally healthy and hardy with few inherent health problems, compared with other breeds. They are, however, high maintenance because they require and demand plenty of your time and attention.

A Lab is not a dog you can put on automatic pilot and let fly on its own until it's convenient for you to spend some time interacting. A Labrador Retriever will not be ignored. You should have chosen a Lab because you are going to incorporate your dog into your life: you like to be outdoors, to go for walks, to play fetch and you want to learn to do obedience work.

A DOG'S SENSES

Sight: With their eyes located farther apart than ours, dogs can detect movement at a greater distance than we can, but they can't see as well up close. They can also see better in less light, but they can't distinguish many colors.

Sound: Dogs can hear about four times better than we can, and they can hear high-pitched sounds especially well. Their ancestors, the wolves, howled to let other wolves know where they were; our dogs do the same, but they have a wider range of vocalizations, including barks, whimpers, moans and whines.

Smell: A dog's nose is his greatest sensory organ. His sense of smell is so great he can follow a trail that's weeks old, detect odors diluted to one-millionth the concentration we'd need to notice them, even sniff out a person under water!

Taste: Dogs have fewer taste buds than we do, so they're likelier to try anything—and usually do, which is why it's especially important for their owners to monitor their food intake. Dogs are omnivores, which means they eat meat as well as vegetable matter like grasses and weeds.

Touch: Dogs are social animals and love to be petted, groomed and played with.

General Characteristics

In my opinion, the Labrador Retriever is the most lovable, even-tempered breed ever developed. Described as a medium-sized sporting dog, the Lab is larger and hardier than the Spaniels of the Sporting Group, and smaller in height but stockier than the Setters and Pointers. The Lab is smaller and has fewer inherent health problems than some of the giant breeds such as the Saint Bernard and the Bernese Mountain Dog. A well-bred Labrador sees everyone as its friend and the world as its oyster. Labradors originally were used to retrieve personal belongings as well as fish that fell off

the hooks and out of the nets of their masters. Over the years, this instinct was fostered, rewarded and encouraged. The early breeders, of course, tried to cement this instinct with careful, selective breeding, so today you will be hard pressed to find a Labrador that does not want to retrieve things or just carry around something in its mouth. Well bred is the key. Where your Labrador comes from can make all the difference in the world.

Lovable Labs make wonderful pals.

As I said in Chapter 2, Labrador Retrievers are very intelligent, which is why they are the most popular breed used today for guiding the blind and for detecting arson, explosives and drugs. They are unflappable as well as intelligent, have a willingness to please and a sturdy constitution. Labradors are also active, bouncy and curious. Eight- to ten-week-old pups will go in spurts. They will have lots of steam and then need to nap like a toddler. They need plenty of exercise and stimulation; they like to be busy! I think the word *busy* really sums up Lab pups. They have lots of energy, and if it's not channeled properly, they'll find something on their own to do that could be destructive. They will dig a big hole or chew a sapling tree down, and then they will be shocked that you are less than delighted. As far as they are concerned, they have made good use of downtime.

Hooked on a Breed

My family got its first two Labs in the early 1960s. They came from Anne Carpenter, a Labrador Retriever and German Shepherd dog breeder. Anne had also been very active in training and running retrievers in trials and in showing. Her Labs came from Mrs. Read's Chidley line.

Ready to play.

Our first, Lobo, was easy to train, quick to learn and easy to entertain. He did very little damage as he was growing up. Though very well bred, he was a bit atypical in that he was often happy doing nothing. Labs like him are the exception, not the rule. His one bad habit was his love of the world outside our fence. He would follow anything or anyone and wind up miles from home. Then, when he was tired, he would lie down on a handy porch and take a nap. He wore an I.D. tag, so it wasn't long before we would get a call from someone who would ask us to come get him.

Discipline Problems: Our second Labrador was an entirely different story. He had no desire to wander far from home, but he was never happy doing nothing. Buffy was a gregarious, beautiful Labrador of excellent breeding with a super temperament. We, however, had been spoiled by our first Labrador and expected Buffy to follow in Lobo's footsteps. This assumption was fatal. When Buffy was about nine months, the family went out for a few hours and left Buffy to entertain himself in the backyard. We came home to find an entire set of redwood patio furniture demolished. Our backyard was a sea of foam stuffing and wood splinters. A few months later, we locked him in the kitchen and went to a party. Buffy had a party of his own. He opened all the lower kitchen cabinets and emptied their contents: pots, pans, paper goods, everything. He chewed the phone off the wall. He opened several tins of my mother's Christmas cookies, ate them and then proceeded to get sick. It wasn't a pretty sight.

These dogs anxiously await their chance to retrieve.

Chewing and destroying things were just part of Buffy's daily routine, but he was so lovable and sweet that it was hard to believe he was guilty of these crimes. I was about ten and often cried myself to sleep sure that he had finally added the straw that would break the proverbial camel's back. Surely my parents would decide to find him a new home, especially because my mother took his getting sick on her Christmas cookies as a personal affront.

Finally, Buffy almost killed himself. While a carpenter was doing some work on our house, Buffy chewed through a live 110-volt extension cord connected to a power saw. The saw stopped and the carpenter went to find the cause. There was Buffy with the severed cord in his mouth, wagging his tail with glee. Somehow, Buffy was fine and very proud of himself. Why he wasn't electrocuted, we'll never know.

Buffy Shapes Up: The lesson we learned from these incidents was that Labs are a breed that needs training and direction from the day they are brought home. With the guidance of Anne Carpenter, we were able to start turning around Buffy's behavior. She came to the house and showed us how to work with Buffy, and she put us in touch with a local obedience trainer and school. This service is but one of the responsibilities of a good, caring breeder. We bought a crate and learned obedience and taught Buffy a routine. We also put up a dog run where the dogs could be contained with shade, water and a few toys. The dog run prevented the dogs from getting into trouble when left unsupervised. There were plenty of toys and room to play but no dangerous objects like shrubbery or wires to chew. Also, *they had each other*. I don't say you need to have more than one Lab, but if you have the space and time, having two is a great idea. (Space them a year or two apart, so they can each have enough special puppy-bonding time.) I don't believe that it's a good idea to raise littermates or two pups that are the same age. They tend to bond to each other more than to you.

CHARACTERISTICS OF THE LABRADOR RETRIEVER

Active

Intelligent, fast learners

Always eager to please

Tendency to chew destructively

Few inherent health problems

Minimal grooming requirements

Demands a high level of attention

Buffy needed to be worked with twice a day, concentrating on the commands "sit," "down," "stay," "come" and "heel" when walked on leash. After our obedience sessions, he needed structured exercise such as fetching a ball or bumper and returning it to hand. Because we intended to show him, we also enrolled in a show-handling class. Buffy turned around 100 percent and became a happy, contented, nondestructive Labrador. The whole family loved him dearly and could now enjoy his company.

Farewell to Friends: We had several happy years together, and we enjoyed their company immensely; they were family. Because of Lobo's sense of adventure, we always kept locks on the gates. One gate was close to the back door; the other was beyond a wooded area not visible from the house. We will never know how or why one rainy autumn night someone unlocked the back gate. When Buffy and Lobo went out before bedtime, they evidently found the open gate. Lobo probably went for a jaunt, and Buffy must have followed him. They were killed about five miles from the house. The police officer who arrived at the scene said that Lobo was hit by a car and killed. A second car hit Buffy, who would not leave Lobo's side. He also was killed.

We were hooked on the breed and could not imagine life without one, two or three Labs. We soon had two more Labs in residence, and many others followed. We named our kennel Lobuff in honor of Lobo and Buffy and think of them fondly and often, especially on rainy autumn nights. The lessons we learned from them were invaluable.

The Importance of Training

In the thirty years that have ensued, my family has bred dozens of litters. Some have become prize-winning show dogs; many others have become cherished family pets, guide dogs for the blind and arson or bomb detectors for the U.S. Bureau of Alcohol, Tobacco and Firearms.

I don't let a puppy go out the door without stressing the importance of training right from the start. With this breed, it's important to establish yourself as the dominant figure from day one. If Labs get the idea even for one minute that they are in charge, you're in for years of unpleasant experiences. You'll be cheating yourself and your Labrador of the wonderful relationship you both deserve. Labradors are big, cuddly teddy bears by nature, and many Labradors think that they're lap dogs even when they reach eighty-five pounds or more. I don't mind their sitting on certain pieces of furniture, but I make it clear from the start which furniture is off-limits.

You must lay down the law right from the start about what is and isn't acceptable behavior. If you let that cute, little eight-week-old puppy on the sofa or in bed with you, at twelve months he will not understand why it's now unacceptable. Never play games like tug-of-war and let him win. Labs are very smart and will not forget this minor victory. A victory of this sort can spur on dominant behavior that you don't want to encourage.

Just as children cannot grow up to be well-adjusted, solid citizens without the help, love and guidance of caring parents, Labradors cannot raise themselves. They're very resourceful animals and will find ways to entertain themselves. Unfortunately, their entertainment may consist of chewing on lawn furniture, uprooting shrubs, digging holes just for fun or digging out of the yard to find companionship. Some of these activities could be dangerous. A Lab must be taught, socialized and loved. A puppy kindergarten class, after the pup's last shots, can be a wonderful learning experience for all.

Best as Buddies

If you're looking for a guard dog, the Labrador isn't the breed for you. They do not have the same protective instinct as a Shepherd or Rottweiler. It is, however, typical of a Lab to bark if someone is outside where he cannot see or if he hears a strange noise. My dogs will bark when a car pulls up the driveway, but once the people enter the house they are greeted and welcomed like family members. My father used to say that if burglars came to our house, the Labs would take them to the silver and then make them a cup of tea. This

This Lab displays a keen sense of smell.

friendly temperament is the most wonderful aspect of the breed and is one of the reasons they are so popular as family dogs. Put simply, they make good buddies.

Again, good breeding is the key. Even though your Lab may accidentally knock over your child or a visiting child with his incredibly strong, jubilant tail, you won't have to worry about him attacking or biting in a protective manner. It's not part of a Lab's makeup. With all the Labradors I've had over the last thirty years, I've never been bitten or had a visitor bitten by one of them. I can't say the same for some other breeds I've owned.

Labradors are active, smart and fast learners. They can be stubborn but can be easily persuaded to see things your way with encouragement and praise. Labradors want to please. They will work eagerly for food rewards but just as eagerly or more for your praise. Corporal punishment is not usually necessary, and, in fact, I strongly discourage it. They love to have something to carry around, and playing fetch is usually a favorite game. I can attest to the fact that their noses are very keen. Over the years, I have lost a few ducks and chickens from the kitchen counter that were dining room bound but never made it due to heavy Labrador traffic through the kitchen. Their eyesight and hearing are also highly developed, but their noses seem to be their guiding force. Whether in the air or on the ground, their noses are always working.

This search dog waits for his handler's signal to "search."

MORE INFORMATION ON LABRADOR RETRIEVERS

NATIONAL BREED CLUB

Labrador Retriever Club, Inc.
Mr. Christopher G. Wincek, Corresponding Secretary
9690 Wilson Mills Road
Chardon, OH 44024

The club can give you information on all aspects of the breed, including the names and addresses of breed, obedience and hunting clubs in your area. Inquire about membership.

BOOKS

Beckett, Diana. *Pet Owner's Guide to the Labrador Retriever.* New York: Howell Book House, 1994.

Churchill, Janet I. *The New Labrador Retriever.* New York: Howell Book House, 1995.

Coode, Carole. *Labrador Retrievers Today.* New York: Howell Book House, 1993.

Howe, Dorothy, with Anna Katherine Nicholas. *The Labrador Retriever.* Neptune, N.J.: TFH Publications, 1984.

Nicholas, Anna Katherine. *The Book of the Labrador Retriever.* Neptune, N.J.: TFH Publications, 1983.

Rutherford, Clarice. *Retriever Puppy Training: The Right Start for Hunting.* Loveland, Colo.: Alpine Publications, 1988.

Rutherford, Clarice, Barbara Branstad, and Sandy Whicker. *Retriever Working Certificate Training.* Loveland, Colo.: Alpine Publications, 1988.

Spencer, James. *Training Retrievers for Marshes & Meadows.* Middleburg, Va.: Denlinger, 1991.

Warwick, Helen. *The New Complete Labrador Retriever.* New York: Howell Book House, 1986.

Magazines

Labrador Quarterly
Hoflin Publishing, Inc.
4401 Zephyr Street
Wheat Ridge, CO 80033-3299

Videos

Field Testing Your Retriever, The AKC Hunting Tests for Retrievers. The American Kennel Club.

Labradors. The American Kennel Club.

With Courage and Style: The Field Trial Retriever. The American Kennel Club.

Living

with a

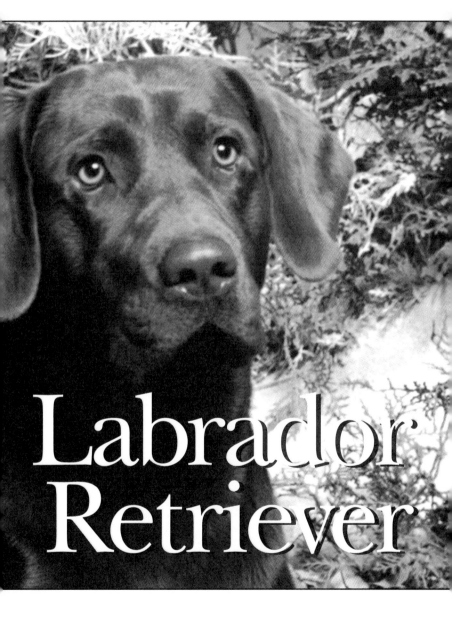

part two

Labrador Retriever

4

Bringing your
Labrador
Retriever
Home

What your new Labrador puppy will need most from you is your time and understanding. Plan to bring your puppy home when you have ample time to spend on acclimating her to her new surroundings. Remember, until the day you bring her home, Sunny will have had the security of her mother and littermates.

When you take your puppy for a checkup, and you should do so as soon as possible after getting her, your veterinarian will probably have an opinion on what and how to feed your puppy. If you read this book and a dozen more about the Labrador Retriever, each author will have an opinion on feeding and training. One book you read may contradict another. Every veterinarian will have an opinion. The point is that after you've sifted through all this information, you have to decide on your own course of action. Pick a veterinarian you can work with and trust. Follow your breeder's advice as much as possible. Select a training method, or enroll in a puppy kindergarten (after the pup's last shots at about eighteen weeks). Most of all, be consistent. Don't change foods every few weeks. Don't overwhelm the puppy with too long a training session at too early an age. And don't try six different training methods in two weeks. Your pup may quickly become bored if you overdo the training, or she may get stubborn and rebellious. Be sensible and don't get carried away with your enthusiasm.

Where to Get Your Puppy

If you bought your puppy from a breeder, chances are the breeder will have given you a diet and feeding instructions. Sunny probably will have had her initial shots and a worming.

I believe that you should seek out a puppy from a private breeder who is breeding for the total Labrador. Look for breeders who show their dogs and do some obedience work as well as hunting retriever tests. When looking for a family pet, steer away from dogs bred strictly for fieldwork or field trials. The field trial dogs of today are high-energy dogs and are difficult, if not impossible, in a home environment.

Remember, the Labrador Retriever you buy now will be part of your family for many years. The more informed you are before making your final decision, the happier you will be when you bring your new puppy home. Look in dog magazines, go to dog shows to watch the Labrador Retrievers compete and talk to their owners. This way, you will be able to make an educated choice when picking your puppy.

Your veterinarian is also a great resource when starting your search. He or she can advise you on what you need to look for in a puppy: bright eyes, healthy skin and coat; normal activity level; and good temperament. You may wish to perform puppy temperament

PUPPY ESSENTIALS

Your new puppy will need:

food bowl

water bowl

collar

leash

I.D. tag

bed

crate

toys

grooming supplies

tests before you make your choice — ask the veterinarian or puppy seller about them.

It's important to see the mother of a litter. She is sometimes referred to as the *dam* or *bitch* in breeder's terms. If your puppy is raised by a pleasant mother dog who has been allowed to play with, discipline and teach her puppy manners, chances are you'll wind up with a nice dog. The mother is really the one who imparts her temperament to the pups. They have their father's or sire's genes and may resemble him in other ways, but males don't often have a hand in the raising of the litter. It's the rare sire that ever sees his pups, so check the dam out carefully, and you'll have fewer problems down the road.

Be wary of a breeder who doesn't let you see the mother—there may be a good reason. Find out what it is. There may be extenuating circumstances—for example, the bitch may be ill. I don't mean to sound distrustful, just cautious. Usually, when people come to see my puppies, they see the dam. They see her interact with her pups, the family and visitors. In the case of a stud dog puppy (the puppy a breeder gets back from a litter sired by his stud dog), you may get to see the sire, or you may have to rely on the breeder to vouch for the characteristics and health of both the sire and the dam. Check out your puppy thoroughly, making sure it's active, friendly and healthy looking, that is, no runny nose or eyes.

If you do your homework before getting your new puppy, you will have many happy years together.

Hunting Dogs: When looking for a companion and family pet that may also be used for hunting, people make the common mistake of searching for a field trial breeder. This type may not yield the best match. Field trial dogs are not necessarily good hunters! Field trials in this country are a very competitive sport, and in time the dogs get better at the tests. The tests get harder, the dogs get better and faster, and the tests again get harder, to the point where they have become very contrived situations with little or no resemblance to an ordinary day's hunting. Instead, look for a breeder who is breeding for a well-rounded Labrador; a well-built, sturdy dog with a willing, pleasant attitude; a dog that will be happy to go out for a day of hunting or retrieving and then equally happy to go home and sleep in front of your fireplace.

The Battle of the Sexes

When people call to inquire about a puppy, I'm often asked, "Which would make a better family pet, a male or a female?" I truly believe that the sex of the puppy should not be the determining factor. I have found Labradors of both sexes to be wonderful companions. People tend to think that males more than females are inclined to roam. This isn't true. Given the chance, dogs of either sex may roam. Because they are friendly and curious, Labs are easily lured away by a passing jogger, by children on their way to school, by ducks on their way to water and by a host of other things. They are not a breed that is easily border-trained to your property like a Collie or German Shepherd dog. Labradors in suburbia need a fenced-in yard or a dog run (a pen at least ten feet by twelve feet), where they will be safe when you're not around. Your Labrador should never be staked or chained on a line with a runner.

Puppy Proofing

It's very important that you puppy proof your house. When you're home and your puppy's housetraining has gotten underway, she must be able to follow you around and learn right from wrong. Tape up electrical cords out of the way because these cords look like fun toys to the Labrador pup. Houseplants pose another danger. Find out if any plants in your house are poisonous; if so, put them high up or do without them for a while. A few common houseplants that are poisonous are English ivy, foxglove, hydrangeas, the rootstalk of the iris plant, lily of the valley, philodendron, dieffenbachia and many ferns. If you suspect that your pup has eaten a poisonous plant, call your veterinarian at once.

Depending on where you live, you may have poisonous plants in your yard or surrounding area that pose a threat to your puppy. Check with your state or local agricultural department about what is native to your area. Where I live, we have lots of mountain laurel and rhododendron that are said to be poisonous if eaten. Luckily, Labradors are hardier than many breeds, and although my dogs have nibbled on the laurel from time to time, only the laurel has suffered. A lot depends on not only the type of plant eaten, but also the amount eaten. In any case, plant eating should be discouraged.

Keep all household cleaning products safely locked up or out of reach. Also, medications, whether canine or human, should be well labeled and kept out of harm's way. Here's another instance when the crate comes in handy. If you go out and forget to put the floor wax away, you won't come home to find Sunny has eaten a quart of it and the plastic bottle it came in if she has been safely locked in her crate.

Toys: Give your puppy toys of her own. There are now almost as many toys for dogs as there are for children. They aren't all safe, so choose carefully. When your

---

HOUSEHOLD DANGERS

Curious puppies and inquisitive dogs get into trouble not because they are bad, but simply because they want to investigate the world around them. It's our job to protect our dogs from harmful substances, like the following:

IN THE HOUSE

cleaners, especially pine oil

perfumes, colognes, aftershaves

medications, vitamins

office and craft supplies

electric cords

chicken or turkey bones

chocolate

some house and garden plants, like ivy, oleander and poinsettia

IN THE GARAGE

antifreeze

garden supplies, like snail and slug bait, pesticides, fertilizers, mouse and rat poisons puppy is in her crate, you may opt for very hard rubber balls or Kong toys because they are virtually indestructible. Sterilized natural bones are also good toys. I like stuffed toys, Booda bones (heavy rope chews and tugs) and squeaky toys, but I only let my puppies have those when supervised. Some toys are great, but since Labrador Retrievers will work on or chew something for hours, not all toys are good crate toys. Labradors will quickly devour chew toys that can be eaten, such as rawhides and pigs' ears. I limit these severely to practically none because these products are often treated with undesirable or unknown chemicals. Given the chance, Labradors will eat pounds of them.

Biscuits: I do give and recommend hard dog biscuits as a treat. I will occasionally give my dogs a big joint or knuckle bone from the butcher, but only after it has been blanched and then only outdoors. The bones are very messy. I don't let my dogs have these bones when they are in a group because a fight may start over them. Labs are not big fighters, but a delicious bone could be a catalyst.

It is a good idea to see how the puppies interact with each other before you select your new pet.

When Labradors are fully grown and totally reliable and trustworthy off leash in the house (usually about ten to fourteen months old, depending on the dog and your training), I let them sleep out of their crates. At this time, I provide them with stuffed cedar beds or washable sheepskin (fake lambskin) rugs. A young pup will often chew and destroy such a bed, but the mature dog appreciates and enjoys it.

41

Housetraining

Labradors are naturally smart and clean. They usually housetrain easily if you are consistent with them. Keep their world small at first. Don't give your puppy the run of the house. Pick a room, like a kitchen or playroom with an easy-to-clean floor and a door to the outside area where you want your puppy to get used to relieving himself. Each time you take the puppy out the door, say "outside, good puppy." Let him relieve himself, and then praise him profusely with "good puppy, good puppy!" in a high-pitched, happy voice.

Supplies

You will need the following equipment: a collar, an identification tag, a leash, water and food bowls, a crate, some toys, perhaps an exercise pen and definitely a set of pooper scoopers. All these items should be available at pet supply stores or through one of the many pet supply mail-order catalogs. Most catalogs have 800 numbers.

The world is a huge place for a small puppy.

Collars: I prefer the rolled (or round leather) collar or a flat nylon collar with a buckle. They come in a variety of colors and designs. The rolled leather collars do

not seem to mess up the hair around the neck as much as the flat ones do, but both are good. I never advise using a choke collar unless your puppy is older and you're enrolled in an obedience class where the instructor wants you to work with one during the training session. Never let a puppy, or a dog, for that matter, run while wearing a live choke collar. By live I mean set up so that it works like a hangman's noose. Sunny could get caught on something in the woods, in the house or even in a car and choke herself to death. Choke collars can be very dangerous, as the name implies, and should be used judiciously. A young Labrador can easily be taught to walk beside you without your using a choke collar.

A pronged or spiked collar is never recommended: A well-bred Labrador shouldn't need one. Some trainers, however, resort to using one far too quickly. These collars are harsh and unnecessary. If you use these measures when Sunny is young, what methods will you need to use when she is eighty-five or ninety pounds? Shock collars? Begin training on the right foot, and you won't need such awful methods.

Identification: Attach an identification tag with your address and telephone number to the collar. Add Sunny's rabies tag after she has had her rabies shot.

Many veterinarians offer tattooing or can tell you where this service is available. Often local breed

Even energetic puppies need to take a break sometimes!

and all-breed clubs offer tattoo clinics, where you can have a tattoo done inexpensively. A dog, however, is not usually tattooed until fully grown. If you tattoo the skin while the dog is a pup, the skin will stretch as she grows, and the tattoo will become illegible. Tattoos are usually done on the inside of the dog's thigh. Most breeders have their stock tattooed. Some of my dogs are tattooed with *L* for Lobuff, my kennel name, and then a number (e.g., L10, L11). Others also have my telephone number. You can also have your dogs tattooed with your Social Security number and registered with the National Registry for a small fee. If your dog is ever lost or stolen and picked up by a pound or laboratory, they will check for a tattoo. If the dog is tattooed with your Social Security number, they will call the National Registry, and they in turn will call you. It's against the law for a laboratory to keep or use a tattooed dog for experimental purposes.

Another option for identification is to have your veterinarian implant (by injection) a chip the size of a grain of rice into your dog with the dog's pertinent information. Most veterinary hospitals, town pounds and shelter facilities now have scanners for these chips. If Sunny is lost, and then she turns up at one of these facilities, they will scan her for a chip and check for a tattoo. Microchips may eventually be the method of choice or the required method of identification by the AKC for all breeders and owners.

Leashes: You'll need a leash when your puppy is about three months old. I recommend a four-foot nylon or cotton-webbed leash to use for walks when you start leash training. This way your puppy can't get too far away from you. Don't let her get in the habit of running to the end of the leash and pulling you. Nip it in the bud, or you'll be sorry when she weighs eighty-five pounds and is dragging you down the street! Flexi-leads are great for older trained dogs when you want to take them to a park or exercise area and let them run without letting them off lead.

The pup will not need a jogging suit because a young pup should not go jogging in the formative stages, especially on hard surfaces. Pounding the pavement can put too much stress on the growth plates and joints and can cause orthopedic problems later.

Bowls: You'll need to get one bowl for food and one for water. I recommend that you buy two three-quart stainless-steel bowls. Labradors make toys out of and chew plastic bowls, and you will be constantly replacing them. If you have two stainless-steel bowls, you can leave one down for water all the time, and use the other for food. Stainless steel is chew-proof and easy to clean either in the sink or dishwasher.

Crates: I highly recommend buying a crate and using it for housetraining and traveling. People sometimes ask, "Don't you think a crate is cruel?" The answer to that is yes if the crate is used incorrectly: Used as a prison, crating is cruel; used wisely, crating is invaluable. Dogs instinctively like to have a little den of their own. They rarely sleep right out in the middle of a room. Usually, they will curl up on something, under something or next to a piece of furniture. The contact gives them a secure feeling. The crate provides that little den that they seek. I prefer the airline type of crate (rigid plastic box with ventilation holes) for housetraining and car travel. It's more like a little dog house. I like the more open wire crate for crating and traveling in warm weather.

When you bring home your new puppy, set up the crate in your bedroom. Sunny will feel safe and secure knowing you are there, but she'll be confined and unable to do damage to your room or to herself. If you only use the crate for sleeping at night and for when no one is home, your puppy will housetrain more quickly. She won't want to soil her sleeping quarters. When you go out, she'll be safe from eating or getting into something dangerous or expensive.

Just like children, puppies appreciate toys and play areas.

Exercise Pens: An exercise pen (similar to a playpen, made of metal, available from pet suppliers) can come in handy. One that is three or four feet high and six or eight feet wide gives you another safe place to put your puppy if she has to be left unsupervised awhile. A pen isn't a replacement for a crate but is to be used in conjunction with a crate. A pen is portable and can be used in the yard or for traveling. If you live in an apartment and don't have a fenced-in yard but do have an available outside area, an exercise pen may be a way for your pup to get some additional fresh air. You must be careful because an exercise pen isn't escape-proof.

Poop Scoops: Poop scoops are a necessity, whether you live in the city or country. Cleaning up after your dog is very important. Viruses as well as internal parasites are transmitted through feces. When a dog defecates at curbside and your pup comes along and sniffs the area, she could pick up a virus or worms. There is a "pooper scooper law" in many cities, but people don't always clean up as well as they should. Keep your puppy away from "busy" curbsides. It's equally important to keep your yard clean, especially if you have other dogs coming through your yard.

Feeding
your
Labrador
Retriever

Every dog needs to be fed appropriately for his age and level of stress and exercise. Most quality foods come in puppy, adult, maintenance, high-test or performance for skin and coat problems and senior or light form.

When to Feed

Some people free feed—leaving food in a bowl, available to the dog at all times, allowing the dog to eat whatever he feels is the right amount. If this method works for you, I think it's fine, but I have so many dogs on different forms of food that I would not be able to keep track of who was eating what, so I feed all my grown dogs twice a day. I think that's the best method for Labs. They are a mouthy breed and are prone to destructive chewing, so I don't recommend just one feeding a day. I believe that some of the chewing they do is

47

from nerves or hunger frustration. It's a well-known fact that Labradors like to eat. Eating just once every twenty-four hours seems to be too much to ask of them! I find my dogs are happier and less likely to get into trouble when they eat twice a day.

Young pups need to eat small amounts over a day, just as a human baby does. The pups' stomachs are small

and cannot take in the amount of food they need for the whole day all at once.

Some puppies will start turning up their noses at one meal or another, and you'll know it's time to go to two meals a day. You know it's time to in-crease the amount of

A group of hun-gry puppies chow down.

food if, when you put it down, Willy gobbles it up and acts frantic (running about looking for more). You'll have to decrease the number of meals but increase the amount at each meal somewhere in that three- to four-month-old stage. I recommend two cups or two and one-half cups twice a day at about four months. Generally, I keep my dogs on puppy food until they are six to eight months old. Every puppy grows differently: some bloodlines mature early and some are very slow to mature. You and your veterinarian must decide when Willy is ready to switch to adult food.

What to Feed

Basically, if you feed a good-quality food, your dog will be getting a balanced diet. Labrador Retrievers are usually good eaters, so it's easy for you to put down a well-balanced meal in one bowl. Avoid the gimmicky stuff that looks like meat or hamburgers or food that makes its own gravy. These types are loaded with preservatives and red dyes. It would be like giving your child hot dogs and candy as a steady diet just because that was what he liked. You wouldn't do it to your child, so don't do it to your Labrador.

As I said, Labs are known for their appetites, so it's rare that any food is left after feeding time. Make sure to note Willy's normal eating habits. If you know what is normal, it's easier to notice when something is abnormal. If he goes off his food for two or more meals, he could be ill. You should take his temperature and have a good look in his mouth to see if perhaps there is a tooth problem. Sometimes, dogs coming down with kennel cough or sore throats go off their feed. If the problem is a twenty-four-hour episode and his appetite returns to normal after a day, you have nothing to worry about. If he continues to refuse food and water, consult your veterinarian.

You should be careful of additives in dog foods, just as in human foods and snacks, so I prefer food that is preserved with vitamin E rather than BHA, BHT or Ethoxoquin. Cancer is on the rise in dogs, so it makes sense to take a good look at the ingredients and preservatives in their food. Cancer is another reason that I don't feed "doggie junk food." At the other extreme, I have had problems with totally "natural" foods. They spoil easily because of a short shelf life, resulting in intestinal problems.

Many good dry foods are designed for every stage of your dog's life. There are also special formulas for dogs that have allergies, are overweight, and so forth. You should select a dry variety that matches your dog's situation, and make sure to try the food for at least a month. If Willy is eating away, you have your food!

> ## HOW MANY MEALS A DAY?
>
> Individual dogs vary in how much they should eat to maintain a desired body weight—not too fat, but not too thin. Puppies need several meals a day, while older dogs may only need one. Determine how much food keeps your adult dog looking and feeling her best. Then decide how many meals you want to feed with that amount. Like us, most dogs love to eat, and offering two meals a day is more enjoyable for them. If you're worried about overfeeding, make sure you measure correctly and abstain from adding tidbits to the meals.
>
> Whether you feed one or two meals, only leave your dog's food out for the amount of time it takes her to eat it—10 minutes, for example. Freefeeding (when food's available any time) and leisurely meals encourage picky eating. Don't worry if your dog doesn't finish all his dinner in the allotted time. He'll learn he should.

I put my puppies on solid food at about three and one-half weeks old, starting with baby rice cereal mixed with warm water, for five days to one week. After that, I mix the cereal with evaporated milk and jarred baby meat (lamb or chicken). I slowly wean them to puppy food, at first mixing it with the baby cereal. They are then fed puppy food with warm water and a jar of baby-food meat, chicken or lamb, three times a day. The timing of this all depends on the size of the litter and the dam's ability to keep up with the demand. I start feeding a large litter earlier than a small one. Pups in a large litter may need to eat four times a day for a while to keep satisfied. It's certainly not an exact science; every breeder has his or her own way of doing it.

Inactive Labradors tend to put on excess weight very quickly. You must monitor and adjust food according to their activity level and nutritional needs. You must also remember that if you are giving between-meal treats such as biscuits (those cute little, hot dog look-alikes or beef jerky strips have no nutritional value, so I don't buy them), a couple of large biscuits add up to another one-half cup or so of food. You must account for this when you are deciding how much food to feed your dog daily.

A Lab's frame should be well covered with coat as well as body substance. A lot of fat is not good for your dog. The right combination of diet and exercise will keep your dog at the proper weight. You must monitor the situation

HOW TO READ THE DOG FOOD LABEL

With so many choices on the market, how can you be sure you're feeding the right food for your dog? The information's all there on the label—if you know what you're looking for.

Look for the nutritional claim right up top. Is the food "100% nutritionally complete?" If so, it's for nearly all life stages; "growth and maintenance," on the other hand, is for early development; puppy foods are marked as such, as are senior foods.

Ingredients are listed in descending order by weight. The first three or four ingredients will tell you the bulk of what the food contains. Look for the highest-quality ingredients, like meats and grains, to be among them.

The Guaranteed Analysis tells you what levels of protein, fat, fiber and moisture are in the food, in that order. While these numbers are meaningful, they won't tell you much about the quality of the food. Nutritional value is in the dry matter, not the moisture content. In many ways, seeing is believing.

If your dog has bright eyes, a shiny coat, a good appetite and a good energy level, chances are his diet's fine. Your dog's breeder and your veterinarian are good sources of advice if you're still confused.

carefully month to month because his dietary needs can change from season to season as well as from year to year. If Willy doesn't spend a lot of time outside in the winter running and expending calories, cut back

on his rations. If he's often outside in the snow bounding through drifts, he may need a bit more food. Be observant. I believe hip dysplasia and other orthopedic problems can be inherited, but they can also be brought on or exacerbated by diet and lack of or too much exercise. (See Chapter 7 for more on orthopedic problems.) Puppies need to be exercising on surfaces where they have good traction. During their developmental stages if they are slipping and sliding and overweight to boot, don't be surprised if problems arise.

Supplements

I give my dogs a multivitamin daily, and I give 1,500 to 2,000 mg of vitamin C to dogs under stress and to those who are in *whelp* (pregnant). Three times a week each dog gets about one-quarter cup of plain yogurt with live cultures. Also, I scramble a bunch of eggs and feed everyone about a one-quarter-cup portion twice a week. I never feed raw eggs to the dogs. If I had a farm and my own chickens, I'd probably feel differently. But I don't, so I scramble or boil the eggs.

Aside from giving puppies evaporated milk for a week or so and giving all my dogs a small amount of plain yogurt, I don't usually feed other dairy foods except for the occasional piece of cheese as a treat or reward. If

---

TYPES OF FOODS/TREATS

There are three types of commercially available dog food—dry, canned and semimoist—and a huge assortment of treats (lucky dogs!) to feed your dog. Which should you choose?

Dry and canned foods contain similar ingredients. The primary difference between them is their moisture content. The moisture is not just water; it's blood and broth, too, the very things that dogs adore. So while canned food is more palatable, dry food is more economical, convenient and effective in controlling tartar buildup. Most owners feed a 25% canned/ 75% dry diet to give their dogs the benefit of both. Just be sure your dog is getting the nutrition he needs (you and your veterinarian can determine this).

Semimoist food has the flavor dogs love and the convenience owners want. However, they tend to contain excessive amounts of artificial colors and preservatives.

Dog treats come in every size, shape and flavor imaginable, from organic cookies shaped like postmen to beefy chew sticks. Dogs seem to love them all, so enjoy the variety. Just be sure not to overindulge your dog. Factor treats into her regular meal sizes.

you're feeding a good, professional-quality food, your dog is getting enough fat and protein. Extra dairy, like a bowl of milk, may add too much fat and is likely to give your dog diarrhea.

At the Dinner Table

My dogs are taught to be well behaved at mealtime, right from the start. Though a Labrador is more convenient than a dust buster for those stray crumbs, peas and so forth, we never hand them food or give in to their begging at the table. They know what's expected of them, and they lie patiently, waiting and watching. Their greatest hope is that the children will be sloppy and let some tidbits fall.

If you are feeding a group of puppies, make sure you have a large enough bowl.

Labradors are usually too dignified to sit up and beg on their hind legs like some other dogs do. Labs are more apt to have their noses up to the table or in your lap. They will nose around between your legs and feet and will be annoying in general if they are not taught to lie down during dinner. It's all up to you. If you let Willy think it's okay to nose around and beg, he will. If you teach him the sit, down and stay commands and give the commands when you sit at the table, he will accept and obey.

Feeding from the table will skew your dog's routine. You may inadvertently feed Willy too much, and he may become overweight. Also, some foods can upset his stomach. You should never feed spicy or greasy foods, and you should be particularly cautious never to feed chocolate because some dogs are fatally allergic to it.

Possible Problems

If your dog develops an allergy or skin problem, your veterinarian may recommend a prescription diet in a can or a dry food specifically formulated for skin problems. There is a prescription diet formulated for just about any problem your dog may have, including special diets for kidney, liver and intestinal problems. These diets are prescribed by your veterinarian after

conclusive tests that show a problem with a specific organ or system. If your dog is going to be on one of these formulas long term, it would be more cost-effective to buy these products by the case. Your veterinarian or specialty supply dealer can order them for you.

I believe you should find a food that seems to agree with your dog and stick with it unless problems arise or your dog's lifestyle changes drastically. The worst thing you can do is switch back and forth, trying this food and that, buying one brand this week because you have a coupon and another brand the fol-

---

TO SUPPLEMENT OR NOT TO SUPPLEMENT?

If you're feeding your dog a diet that's correct for her developmental stage and she's alert, healthy-looking and neither over- nor underweight, you don't need to add supplements. These include table scraps as well as vitamins and minerals. In fact, a growing puppy is in danger of developing musculoskeletal disorders by oversupplementation. If you have any concerns about the nutritional quality of the food you're feeding, discuss them with your veterinarian.

---

lowing week. The dog's intestinal flora do not adjust to new foods or food changes the way a human's do. You'll be better off sticking to one brand unless Willy is not thriving on his diet. I like to try a new food for at least one month before I decide how the dog is doing on it. If, however, Willy has an allergic reaction or if the food causes vomiting, diarrhea or abstinence, reevaluate the situation sooner.

The moral of this story is buy a good food, feed it correctly, check stools yearly (see Chapter 7 for more information) and your Labrador Retriever should thrive.

6

Grooming
your
Labrador
Retriever

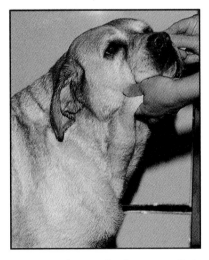

If you are a new Lab owner or about to become one, you will discover that they need only minimal coat care. The Labrador's natural coat is pretty much wash and wear. Even if your lovely Lab, Sunny, has been out in the rain and mud, a toweling, followed by a brushing when she's dry, should restore that beautiful coat. You can bathe your Labrador if she's really filthy, has fleas or has gone out for a romp and rolled in something pungent like horse manure. As a rule, however, Labs don't need much bathing. They have a natural oil to their coats, and too much bathing strips the coat of it. Even Labs that are show dogs get very few baths. Often, I stop at a nearby river on my way to a dog show, let the dogs have a quick swim, towel them dry a bit, and it's off to the dog show!

The Labrador can withstand very cold water because of its double coat. As I said before, the Labrador has a thick undercoat under a harsh-feeling topcoat. The texture of the coat does differ from color to color. Coats on the blacks and chocolates are usually a bit more harsh, although I occasionally see a yellow with an exceptional coat. The blacks' and chocolates' coats can get sunburned; the chocolates are the most susceptible to bleaching from the sun.

Shedding

Bitches will usually shed out twice a year. Their hair growth and shedding are a consequence of hormonal changes. Bitches are usually in full bloom coat just before coming into season; two or three months later, they usually molt. Females will generally have beautiful coats throughout a pregnancy and then lose all their hair down to their skin just about the time their pups are ready to go to their new homes.

A well-groomed Labrador Retriever looks stately.

Males as well as spayed females usually have one big shed-out in the spring and a smaller hair loss in the autumn. Sometimes, coats get more harsh and profuse with age. Coat quality is largely a product of genetics, but the coat is also affected by climate, living conditions and diet. A Labrador that's not out in the cool or cold, damp weather, at least part of the year, usually will not develop the same coat as a dog that's exposed to the cool or damp weather. Labs that spend the majority of their time in a house with dry heat seem to constantly shed a little bit of hair and don't develop good coats. Labs that are in the house most of the time often have itchy, flaky skin. You can add wheat germ oil or a tablespoon of butter to their rations or ask your veterinarian to recommend something. A product called Derm Caps seems to work well. If the problem persists, you might try a food specially formulated for skin and coat.

Brushing

I like to use a good, strong nylon or natural bristle brush, once or twice a week on the coat. You can also roll up a rough towel and buff the coat. Start up by Sunny's neck and pull the towel down toward the tail. Labradors love the attention that comes with grooming, and they usually cooperate.

Put your dog on a grooming table or other raised surface to prevent straining your back when you groom. Sunny will still have a good grooming if she lies on the

floor and you sit down with her. Have her roll over so that you can do one side and then the other. I don't use a comb or slicker brush for daily care. You should only use them when it's time for the coat to come out and it's coming out by the handful when you touch your dog. If the coat is coming out anyway, I

Puppies, as well as adults, benefit from routine grooming.

suggest helping it along. The idea is to change the coat as quickly as possible. You want to get rid of the dead coat so that the new coat grows in properly. At this time, a few warm baths also help to speed the process. A warm bath with a mild shampoo followed by a rough toweling and then a combing or a brushing with a slicker brush will be a big help. If you give these baths three weeks in a row, the bulk of the hair that's coming out will be out. Also, you won't be pulling your own hair out because you have to vacuum twice a day and are wearing Labrador hair all over your clothes. All this happens for a very short time. Be glad it's not Shepherd or Collie hair!

For general care, a good brushing a few times a week and a wipe and shine with a chamois cloth or towel will make Sunny's coat look just fine. It is, however, a good idea to buy a flea comb. This is a special comb with teeth so close together that the fleas and flea dirt are trapped, and you can comb them right off the dog and into a pan of alcohol. You won't be able to get a flea comb through a Labrador Retriever in full coat, but in the summer and autumn (flea season), when Labs are basically out of coat, you can use this comb to detect and help rid the dog of fleas.

If you come across a tick when you're brushing, you can use tweezers to pull it out. Make sure you pull out the head of the tick by pinching with the tweezers as close as possible to the body. Apply antiseptic to the bite site. Dispose of the tick carefully by dropping it from the tweezers into alcohol. (The American dog tick transmits Rocky Mountain spotted fever. The deer tick transmits Lyme disease. See Chapter 7 for examples of ticks.)

If you have a flea problem, I recommend adding garlic and brewer's yeast to the dog's food. Mixtures of garlic and brewer's yeast are readily available in pet supply stores and through pet catalogs. I don't use flea collars, sprays, powders or dips unless they are herbal. When you use products with pesticides and poisons, they can be absorbed through the dog's skin, your skin and your children's as well. I would not let my child wear a poison necklace around his or her neck, and I don't let my dogs wear them either.

As I mentioned in Chapter 5, with more and more dogs getting cancer, you really have to be careful with pesticides. Often, when people find fleas, their first reaction is to call an exterminator, have the house flea bombed, spray the yard, dip the dog, powder the dog and put a flea collar on her! If the fleas resurface, which often happens, many people go through the same routine again. Just think of how much poison is

GROOMING TOOLS

pin brush

slicker brush

flea comb

towel

matt rake

grooming glove

scissors

nail clippers

tooth-cleaning equipment

shampoo

conditioner

clippers

being sprayed around and being inhaled or absorbed by everyone, not just the dog. Do this year after year and you could be shortening your life and your dog's as well.

Everyone hates fleas and ticks, and certain areas seem to be plagued by them. If you live near woods or sandy soil and the summer is warm and damp, the fleas can really get a foothold. If you don't have a hard freeze until November or December, the flea season can seem endless. Worms and worming will be discussed in Chapter 7, but it's important to note now that fleas transmit tapeworm. After you get rid of the fleas you must get rid of the tapeworm.

With patience and a consistent approach, your dog will gladly allow you to trim her nails.

Labs of all three colors can be bothered by fleas, but sometimes it does seem that the light yellows have more sensitive skin (like fair-haired people). Some dogs are very flea allergic, and it's painful to watch them scratch and suffer. If severe, the situation may warrant a trip to the vet. The vet may prescribe a cortisone derivative to give the dog some relief. Unfortunately, fleas are a fact of life, or life with a pet, but take heart: flea season doesn't last all year.

Trimming the Coat

Labradors don't require any hair trimming. They look their best in their natural, untrimmed state. Unlike Poodles and Terriers, they don't need to go to the professional groomer unless they need a bath and you cannot manage one at home. Of course, there is always the garden hose in nice weather.

Trimming the Nails

Your Labrador's nails should be trimmed so that you cannot hear them clicking on the floor. When you buy a nail clipper, I recommend the large dog-pliers type or the guillotine type. It's really a matter of preference, so use what makes you feel most comfortable. There are several good brands on the market. Start good nail care when your puppy is young so that she will become accustomed to the procedure. Make nail clipping a part of your grooming routine every ten days to two weeks. I don't remove the dewclaws on my

dogs. The dewclaw is the prehensile toe up on the inside front legs. You'll have to pay particular attention to trimming these claws because they don't wear down when your dog is walking or running. They only touch the ground when your dog uses them to climb up a bank coming out of a river, lake or such. They can grow completely around, almost in a circle, and stick into the dog's leg, causing much pain. Always check to make sure they are kept short.

If Sunny goes for regular walks on pavement or runs back and forth on a cement dog run, the four front and rear nails will be fairly

worn down, and you'll probably just need to clip the ends of the nails. You should try not to clip the nail too short and cut the quick because it will bleed profusely and be painful. The quick is easier to see on yellow Labs than on black or chocolate Labs. If you constantly cut the quick, your Lab will not only feel pain, but also be uncooperative for her pedicure.

Good grooming entails more than just brushing and bathing—don't forget the teeth, ears and eyes!

To get a pup used to the routine of nail clipping, I start in the following way: I sit on the floor and hold the pup on her back on my lap (head toward me) and do the front nails, then I turn the pup around (still on her back but with her tail toward me) and clip the back nails. I have known people who have had to take their dog to the veterinarian to have its nails clipped, sometimes under sedation, because they neglected to trim its nails regularly when the dog was young. Left untrimmed, long nails can cause the dog's feet to splay (toes spread apart), cause the dog to slip and slide on hard surfaces and cause the dog discomfort.

Some breeders I know prefer an electric nail grinder (or drummel). Puppies need to get used to this device at a fairly young age because the noise can scare them. You can also use a file. Some people who are afraid to clip the nails prefer a file because you can file gradually and are less likely to hit the quick. This procedure takes a bit longer, however, so your dog has to be very willing to cooperate.

Teeth

A large dog biscuit once a day is good for your dog's teeth. In conjunction with her dry kibble, it will help keep her teeth clean. You'll also find chew toys like Nylafloss and Gumabones can help to keep tartar and plaque down.

Eyes

Occasionally, yellow Labs get unsightly eye stains that are not necessarily a medical problem. These stains could, however, be the result of blocked tear ducts. Your veterinarian may or may not be able to treat this condition. If these stains are just a cosmetic problem, you can put a drop of mineral oil in each eye and wipe the stains with a cotton ball soaked in hydrogen peroxide. There are some products available in pet supply stores that may also help. Black and chocolate Labradors may tear as well, but you will not notice it because of their dark hair.

Ears

If your dog has an ear infection, it will usually give off a bad odor. You should check her ears weekly or every other week. I wipe out my dogs' ears regularly with an ear cleanser. Using a cotton ball soaked in solution,

I wash around the inside of the ear. I use my index finger to wipe down in the ear canal almost up to the second joint of my finger. If the ear is inflamed and badly infected, you should seek veterinary help because your

dog probably needs medication. Tooth, eye and ear care are covered more fully in Chapter 7.

The most important thing to remember about grooming your Labrador is to make grooming time enjoyable for you and your dog. Consider it bonding or quality time: It's

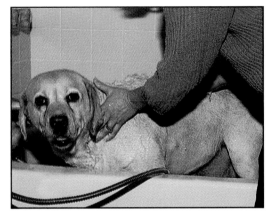

worth the effort. With very little effort, you can keep your Labrador looking as if she just stepped out of the grooming parlor. In reality, she will probably never have to set foot in one.

Routine bathing is actually enjoyable.

chapter 7

Keeping your
Labrador
Retriever
Healthy

A healthy Labrador Retriever is one that is active, alert, well fed, well exercised and well muscled, gets the right amount of food, exercise and rest and is the recipient of good preventive care. The role of preventive medicine in overall health is recognized as invaluable for people, and the adage "an ounce of prevention is worth a pound of cure" is just as true for our dogs.

Prevention Is the Best Cure

Preventive maintenance is a good idea even though the Labrador Retriever is a comparatively low-maintenance breed. You can practice some simple preventive measures for your dog's good health. Your Lab will not require frequent bathing. In fact, doing so can remove too much of the natural oil and can dry out your dog's skin, resulting in flaking and itching. Labs that spend too much time indoors, particularly in the winter months when our houses are drier, are also more susceptible to skin problems. I make sure my dogs spend several hours outside every day. Remember, their thick double coats insulate them well, and they can spend hours outside even on a cold winter day and not feel chilled at all. On the other hand, I don't recommend that they live outside full-time.

You should have a daily routine as well as a weekly or monthly routine and a yearly schedule. Your daily routine might consist of giving Willy a thorough going over with your hands, like a massage. Sit on the floor with him, dig your fingers into that coat and check him from head to toe. Become familiar with the way he feels normally, and you'll be able to quickly spot anything abnormal. In the warm weather, you might find fleas and ticks and can remedy the situation. You may find burrs if you have been out in the woods or on a hike. You will feel any growths or lumps if they crop up. Again, you'll know what Willy usually feels like, so you'll be able to spot the unusual. A tumor or unusual growth should be seen by your veterinarian. It may just be a fatty tumor, but your veterinarian may recommend removing or biopsying it to rule out any cancer or precancerous growths.

Your weekly routine might include checking and cleaning eyes and ears if needed. Depending on the type of terrain your dog walks or runs over, his nails may need a monthly or biweekly clipping.

Vaccinations, heartworm and fecal checks can be on a yearly schedule. Most veterinarians will send you a postcard when your dog is due for boosters and so forth. Make sure to mark the date on your calendar and to make it part of your routine with your dog.

Your Veterinarian

Selecting a veterinarian is an important first step toward establishing routine professional care and making sure help is available in the event of illness or injury. Ask your breeder for a recommendation if you live in the same area. Ask friends who have pets. Assess the practice the way you would assess a physician for yourself and your family. Is the staff courteous and professional? Are appointments available in a reasonable time frame? Are the facilities clean and well maintained? Don't be afraid to ask questions. Sometimes, professionals need to be gently reminded that they must explain themselves in layman's terms. Above all, if at any time your veterinarian says or does something that causes you to be concerned or alarmed, get a second opinion.

WHEN TO CALL THE VET

In any emergency situation, you should call your veterinarian immediately. You can make the difference in your dog's life by staying as calm as possible when you call and by giving the doctor or the assistant as much information as possible before you leave for the clinic. That way, the vet will be able to take immediate, specific action to remedy your dog's situation.

Emergencies include acute abdominal pain, suspected poisoning, snakebite, burns, frostbite, shock, dehydration, abnormal vomiting or bleeding, and deep wounds. You are the best judge of your dog's health, as you live with and observe him every day. Don't hesitate to call your veterinarian if you suspect trouble.

You should schedule your new puppy's first visit to the veterinarian within a day or so of bringing him home, usually around eight to eight and one-half weeks of age. I don't recommend bringing puppies to their new homes before the age of seven to seven and one-half weeks. My puppies typically join their new families around eight or nine weeks of age.

Willy should not need a shot at this time, just a checkup. This first visit is important for many reasons. It sets the stage for your puppy to become comfortable with regular veterinary care. It gives your veterinarian an opportunity to assess your puppy and identify any potential problems early. Your veterinarian will probably want to check Willy's eyes, teeth or dentition, mouth, nose, skin, bone structure and heartbeat. This visit should be a fun visit; therefore, your pup should associate going to the veterinarian with good things, not scary ones. Your puppy probably had a thorough exam like this before you bought him. Your breeder should have given you a list of all inoculations, wormings and medications the pup has had and a veterinary health certificate. In any case, it's good for your peace of mind to have him seen by your veterinarian and double check that all systems are go!

Diet

As discussed in the chapter on feeding, diet is an integral part of your Lab's overall health picture. An undernourished dog lacks energy and will be more susceptible to illness. In general, if your Lab is off his food and water for more than twenty-four to thirty-six hours, you should call your veterinarian. He may want to see your dog. Labradors are voracious eaters, so a Labrador that refuses food for two or more days is probably experiencing some sort of problem.

The proper amount of fat in your dog's diet will also help to keep coat and skin in good condition. Adding a bit of oil such as wheat-germ oil to the food may help. Products that contain fatty acids can also help and are easily found at your pet supply store.

Monitor your dog for signs of dehydration. You can tell if he's dehydrated by pulling his skin away from his body (not too hard); if it snaps right back he's probably okay; if the skin doesn't snap back, he might not be getting enough fluids. You might also want to take your dog's temperature so that if and when you do call your veterinarian, you'll have the answers to the vet's first

A healthy dog can better enjoy the activities for which she was originally bred.

few questions. A dog's temperature is taken with a rectal thermometer. I use alcohol wipes to clean the thermometer between uses. Shake the thermometer down as you would for human use, then dip the end in some Vaseline or A&D ointment. I find it easier to have the dog lie

down, though if he prefers to stand and you can prevent him from sitting for about three minutes, that's okay, too. Insert the thermometer about one inch into the rectum. If you have a clock or watch with a sweep hand, keep an eye on it and leave the thermometer in for about three minutes. Take the thermometer out, wipe it with alcohol and read. Normal temperature for a dog is 100 degrees to 102.5 degrees Fahrenheit. The average is about 101.2 degrees Fahrenheit. For a fever of 104 degrees Fahrenheit or more, call your veterinarian.

Obesity

Watch Willy's weight. As a rule, Labs love to eat, and it's fairly easy to overfeed them. Most healthy Labradors will rarely refuse food. Remember, if you're giving treats like dog biscuits and table scraps, these calories add up. Two large biscuits are equal to about one-half cup of food. If you're going to feed two or more biscuits a day, then cut back accordingly on the kibble at mealtime. An overweight Lab is placing additional stress on vital systems and organs. Excessive weight can be bad for your Lab's heart and particularly bad for his joints and growth plates when he is a growing pup.

Exercise: As they get older and less active, many Labs become increasingly overweight. I advise the owners to gradually cut back on food or switch to a less caloric food. Even an older dog can enjoy a good walk or romp as long as there are no other health problems. I vary my dogs' exercise between swimming, running in the sand, romping over hill and dale and retrieving a ball or bumper. In this way, all the muscle groups get a workout. Labs of all ages need exercise. I like mine to have a morning and an evening romp. Their exercise is part of my daily routine. It's good quality time. Lack of exercise from early adulthood through middle age can lead to problems. Moreover, boredom can set in, and Willy may start getting into mischief reminiscent of his puppy days. Labs that don't have anything to do may start licking their legs out of boredom, which can cause "lick sores." This behavioral problem is one that exercise can help to avoid. A well-exercised dog has a good healthy appetite and can really enjoy that afternoon nap.

Wherever possible, exercise your dog on grass or soft ground and limit the amount of exercise on pavement or asphalt. Although harder surfaces are good for trimming down nails, they are rough on joints, and the friction caused by these surfaces can result in sore or swollen pads. If Willy's pads become raw and cracked, the sore will not only cause pain but also take quite awhile to heal. If this happens, you can use an over-the-counter triple antibiotic ointment on the pads, and try walking your dog with a sock or booty over the open sore to prevent sand and dirt from entering the wound and making it worse. In the wild, a good mud pack would probably have been recommended, but this remedy is not always possible in suburbia or in the city.

Eyes

Labrador eyes should require little care on your part. Periodically, you may wish to gently cleanse around the eye area with a cotton ball soaked in boiled, salted water. As is true in humans, never put anything in your dog's eye that doesn't say it's for ophthalmic use. Yellow Labs may get brown stains because of normal tearing and secretions. This problem is usually cosmetic and can sometimes be remedied by cleansing with a cotton ball soaked with hydrogen peroxide. You don't want to get the peroxide in the eye because it will burn, so put a drop of mineral oil in each eye in case you accidentally get too close to the eye.

Occasionally, your Labrador may develop a blocked tear duct. If there is complete obstruction and tears cannot be adequately drained, your veterinarian may attempt to clear the ducts by flushing them out or clearing the obstruction. Sometimes, the ducts are

---

FIGHTING FLEAS

Remember, the fleas you see on your dog are only part of the problem—the smallest part! To rid your dog and home of fleas, you need to treat your dog *and* your home. Here's how:

• Identify where your pet(s) sleep. These are "hot spots."

• Clean your pets' bedding regularly by vacuuming and washing.

• Spray "hot spots" with a non-toxic, long-lasting flea larvicide.

• Treat outdoor "hot spots" with insecticide.

• Kill eggs on pets with a product containing insect growth regulators (IGRs).

• Kill fleas on pets per your veterinarian's recommendation.

overactive and the dog's eyes tear excessively. If this excessive tearing is being caused by irritation, try to determine what the irritant is and get rid of it.

Dogs can get conjunctivitis and require treatment with an ophthalmic ointment. The whites of the eyes will usually be quite red, and you will see a beige or greenish discharge. This discharge can be profuse and can easily be spread from dog to dog. Careful hand washing is a must! Conjunctivitis may be caused by irritants in the dog's environment, virus or bacteria. Your dog should be seen by your veterinarian to get the proper medication.

To remove a foreign body from the eye, try flushing it gently with water. A sterile saline solution is best. Simply boil some water, add a little salt (about one-half teaspoon to a cup of water), let it cool to room temperature and put some in a cup. Hold your dog's eye open as you flush it out. If you choose a squeeze-type bottle for irrigation, be careful not to use force that could injure the eye. If you are unsuccessful in removing the object because you need help and cannot keep the dog still enough, call your veterinarian before you do damage by poking around the eye as the dog is squirming. Also, certain items may actually be imbedded in the eye and require removal with a tweezer or forceps. Let more experienced hands do the job.

*Squeeze eye oint-
ment into the
lower lid.*

Cataracts can be a problem in Labradors. It's assumed that they are hereditary unless they are the result of some trauma, dietary deficiency or disease such as diabetes. When cataracts completely affect the lenses of both eyes, blindness usually occurs. A cataract is an opacity on the lens and may be found in one or both eyes. Your dog must be seen by a board-certified ophthalmologist to correctly diagnose the kind of cataract and the impact it will have on your dog's vision.

Progressive Retinal Atrophy (PRA): This hereditary eye disease causes blindness. The two types of PRA are CPRA and GPRA. PRA is thought to be inherited, but the mode of inheritance is still being debated. The disease is usually detected at about four years of age, using a slit lamp or ophthalmoscope, but it can be detected by an electroretinogram (ERG) at about 18 months of age. Night blindness is often the first symptom, but over time PRA progresses to complete blindness. This process can take months or a year. Most serious breeders have their breeding stock, ages one year to ten, checked annually by a board certified canine ophthalmologist. After administering eyedrops that dilate the pupils and then waiting fifteen minutes or so, the ophthalmologist examines the eyes with a slit lamp or ophthalmoscope. This procedure identifies cataracts or PRA.

Run your hands regularly over your dog to feel for any injuries.

If no abnormalities are found, the ophthalmologist will so indicate on a form, which the owner can send to Purdue University to the Canine Eye Registration Foundation (CERF). For a small fee, a registration number is assigned. It may be renewed each year after the annual exam. Though there has been much talk lately about diseases such as PRA, the problem isn't as widespread or rampant as some would have you believe. As long as you buy a puppy from a good breeder who checks eyes annually, the likelihood that you will encounter PRA is minuscule. Labs that do go blind later in life due to cataracts or other ocular disorders seem to function very well. Their keen senses of smell and hearing guide them.

Feet

Foot care for Labradors is minimal. The hair on their feet doesn't need trimming, and there is no hair to get iced up in bad weather. Short nails are important to keep their feet from splaying (spreading) and slipping on your floors, creating orthopedic problems.

Labs can be prone to interdigital cysts. These are pea-sized lumps that crop up between the toes. Sometimes an antibiotic helps. You can use a topical ointment or soak the foot in Epsom salts and warm water. Some veterinarians lance the cysts. No matter what treatment you follow, it seems to take about a week to ten days for them to heal! It also seems that if your dog is prone to cysts, the problem will recur throughout his life. Though the cyst itself does not present a serious problem or condition, it's important to keep the area of the cyst clean to avoid infection.

Check your dog's teeth frequently and brush them regularly.

Teeth

You can help to keep your dog's teeth clean by feeding a dry food with crunch, dog biscuits, bones that are safe and cannot splinter and toys that are designed to clean the teeth, like Gumabones or Nylafloss. If plaque does build up and the teeth look stained or smell, you may need your veterinarian to do dentistry. Dentistry is performed under anesthesia.

Muzzling: Rarely does a Labrador bite, but never say never! Any animal can bite, especially an animal in pain. If your Lab is hurt, he may snap out of pain and desperation. It's a good idea to have a muzzle available for an emergency. A simple leather one that buckles behind the ears and around the neck won't hurt the dog and will keep the dog from hurting you, someone else or himself. You can improvise with a leather leash three to four feet long. Wrap the middle section of the leash around the dog's muzzle two to three times (snugly, but not too tight), leaving a piece long enough on either side of the muzzle to pull back and tie around the neck. Again, be careful that it isn't so tight that it chokes the dog or causes breathing problems. It should be just snug enough to keep the teeth in the mouth.

Vaccinations

Inoculations are an integral part of the responsible owner's duties. Just as children's inoculations have prevented once common and sometimes fatal diseases, dogs are living longer and healthier lives thanks to the development of vaccinations against disease. Your veterinarian will probably follow the guidelines set by a veterinary school like Cornell University, suggesting the number of vaccinations required to give adequate coverage. Scheduling may vary a bit from veterinarian to veterinarian. Certain diseases are more prevalent in some parts of the country than in others.

The DA$_2$PL-P series is probably the most routinely given combination of vaccines. DA$_2$PL-P stands for Canine Distemper, Adenovirus-2, Infectious Hepatitus, Parainfluenza, Leptospirosis and Parvovirus-2. These can be given separately but are usually given together. The two most important shots are the first and the last. The first should be given before your pup leaves his breeder (some breeders may have given two shots by the time you take your pup). It's important that the last shot be given at about seventeen or eighteen weeks of age because that's when the mother's immunities will have worn off and immunities from the vaccinations will kick in. The following schedule is the one I follow per my veterinarian: first shot—six and one-half weeks; second shot—nine weeks; third shot—twelve weeks; fourth shot—fifteen weeks; fifth shot—eighteen weeks.

Use a scarf or old hose to make a temporary muzzle, as shown.

These are followed by a rabies vaccination at five or six months of age and by another booster if I'm planning to show him. Your veterinarian's schedule for vaccinations may differ slightly.

The diseases that these inoculations are intended to prevent are discussed in more detail in the following section. You should be aware that while inoculations generally provide protection from illness, it's possible for a pup's system to reject the immunity from the vaccinations or to develop one of these terrible diseases.

I think it is most important not to drag a new pup all over the place when you first take ownership. Take him home and keep him home until he has had his twelve-week shots if you live in the country. If you live in the city, I recommend not taking the pup out to the curb until he has had his fifteen-week shots. It would not be prudent to take a potentially vulnerable pup out to a beach or park where countless other dogs have been that day. These other dogs might have left their germs behind. For the same reason, I recommend that you do not start a training or puppy kindergarten class with other pups until your pup is about sixteen weeks of age.

Distemper: Many veterinarians first give pups a distemper and measles vaccine at about five weeks of age. Because of the viruses, similarities, the measles virus may help give your pup immunity against distemper.

Prevention is key—make sure you keep up-to-date on all your dog's vaccinations.

Getting distemper immunity from the measles vaccine is important because the antibodies the pup has gotten from his mother will sometimes render the distemper vaccine useless. Combining the two will help in the early stages but does not seem to work in older pups over ten or twelve weeks. As the mother's immunities wear off, the standard distemper vaccine becomes effective.

Distemper is a very contagious disease that can move through a colony of pups like a house on fire.

Distemper is typically seen in the spring, affecting dogs from three to six months of age. Symptoms can vary, but usually a fever will be a first sign. Your pup may look as though he has a cold with runny eyes and nose. Dogs do not get the common cold so be suspicious of such symptoms. The pup may also suffer from diarrhea and dehydration. Caught in this first stage, distemper is often successfully treated.

If distemper is not caught early, more serious symptoms may appear such as drooling, chomping at the air (as if trying to catch a fly) and head shaking. He may also act as if he's trying to spit out something. Externally, you may see pustules on the skin of his underside. If the disease affects the brain, the next sign may be seizures. Your dog may stiffen and fall over or flail his legs about. If the disease gets to this point, survival is unlikely. Early detection of this disease is critical for survival.

Treatment depends on the symptoms. There is no antibiotic for the virus, though one may be given to fight possible secondary bacterial infections that are often a cause of death. Usually, a dog is given the shotgun treatment: fluids given subcutaneously and intravenously to control the diarrhea and dehydration. The dog may be given Dilantin or Phenobarbital for the seizures and possibly a sedative.

> ## YOUR PUPPY'S VACCINES
>
> Vaccines are given to prevent your dog from getting an infectious disease like canine distemper or rabies. Vaccines are the ultimate preventive medicine: they're given before your dog ever gets the disease so as to protect him from the disease. That's why it is necessary for your dog to be vaccinated routinely. Puppy vaccines start at eight weeks of age for the five-in-one DHLPP vaccine and are given every three to four weeks until the puppy is sixteen months old. Your veterinarian will put your puppy on a proper schedule and will remind you when to bring in your dog for shots.

Infectious Canine Hepatitis: This virus is also very contagious. It is a different viral form of hepatitis from the one that affects people, although some of the same organs are involved, such as the liver and the kidneys. It can be spread through contact with contaminated feces, urine and saliva. The disease can be diagnosed with a blood test.

Symptoms are often similar to those of distemper. The dog may spike a fever of 105 degrees Fahrenheit to 106 degrees Fahrenheit. He will refuse food and water and be very lethargic. He may vomit and have bloody diarrhea. He may be very sensitive to light. Due to liver involvement, he may have a painful abdomen. Jaundice may set in, and you may notice that the whites of the eyes are yellowish. There are strains that have a sudden onset of severe symptoms, and a dog or puppy succumbs quickly. Get a dog or pup with these symptoms to your veterinarian without delay. Most are treated with IV fluids, rest, warmth and antibiotics for secondary bacterial infections. Occasionally, blood transfusions are necessary. The mortality rate is quite high. Keeping Willy up to date on his hepatitis vaccine is the best way to prevent this devastating disease.

Parvovirus: Commonly known as Parvo, the virus is a big killer of puppies in most breeds as well as in Labs. Because Labs are hardy, I have seen many pull through severe cases of Parvo. Parvo is a gastro-intestinal virus that attacks the lining of the intestines and causes bloody diarrhea that has a distinct foul odor. The virus is extremely contagious and can sweep through a kennel or shelter with deadly force. Pups or adult dogs can die in as little time as forty-eight hours. The key to saving dogs or pups is *early detection*. Patients need to be treated quickly with fluids, IV, antibiotics, rest and warmth. If Willy rapidly develops bloody diarrhea (and

IDENTIFYING YOUR DOG

It's a terrible thing to think about, but your dog could somehow, someday, get lost or stolen. How would you get him back? Your best bet would be to have some form of identification on your dog. You can choose from a collar and tags, a tattoo, a microchip or a combination of these three.

Every dog should wear a buckle collar with identification tags. They are the quickest and easiest way for a stranger to identify your dog. It's best to inscribe the tags with your name and phone number; you don't need to include your dog's name.

There are two ways to permanently identify your dog. The first is a tattoo, placed on the inside of your dog's thigh. The tattoo should be your social security number or your dog's AKC registration number.

The second is a microchip, a rice-sized pellet that's inserted under the dog's skin at the base of the neck, between the shoulder blades. When a scanner is passed over the dog, it will beep, notifying the person that the dog has a chip. The scanner will then show a code, identifying the dog. Microchips are becoming more and more popular and are certainly the wave of the future.

sometimes vomiting) with an awful odor, call your veterinarian or emergency hospital immediately! Don't wait! Pups are vaccinated against Parvo, but the vaccination is not absolute protection.

Coronavirus: This virus also has a vaccine. It is shed in the stool and is more likely to be fatal to a pup than to an otherwise healthy adult. Symptoms of this virus include bloody diarrhea, vomiting, lethargy and lack of appetite. The stool may also be watery, yellow and mucus-like. There is no antibiotic for coronavirus. It's important to control the vomiting and diarrhea because they can lead to dehydration. Your veterinarian may give you fluids to replace electrolytes, or you can get Pedialyte at a drugstore where baby formulas are sold. Most likely, your veterinarian will want to keep your puppy on IV. I recommend getting this vaccine, but again, I believe isolating Willy from others until he is older is important.

Leptospirosis: This disease, commonly called Lepto, is bacterial. The bacteria are shed in the urine of many wild animals. If you are out for a hike and Willy sniffs at a tree or bush on which an infected animal has urinated, he can contract the disease. He can also get it from drinking contaminated water from a puddle or pond that has been urinated in by an infected animal. Lepto is very contagious to humans as well as to dogs. It attacks the kidneys and liver and is often fatal.

Symptoms usually start with loss of appetite and fever. These symptoms are sometimes accompanied by diarrhea and jaundice; the whites of the eyes will look yellow. Antibiotics are used, but this serious disease is hard to combat. Because Lepto is not prevalent all over the country, not all dogs are vaccinated. If you will be traveling out of your hometown to an area where Lepto is found, your Lab should be vaccinated.

Tracheobronchitis: This disease, often referred to as "kennel cough," can be bacterial or viral. The contagions are airborne and can cause many symptoms other than the hacking cough. This is a respiratory infection that can cause inflammation of the lungs, bronchi and trachea. The cough can be mild or severe, and the dogs may go off their feed. Usually, an antibiotic will be given to stave off secondary infections such as pneumonia.

Vaccines are available and can be given by injection or intranasally. They are a good idea especially if you're going to be boarding Willy at a kennel, taking him to a groomer for a bath or going to indoor dog shows. Usually, kennel cough is mild, lasts about a week and can be controlled with a cough suppressant. Your veterinarian may recommend an over-the-counter product usually used by humans.

Healthy puppies enjoy playing together.

Rabies: It's very important to vaccinate against rabies. This highly infectious viral disease affects the central nervous system. It is deadly and can be transmitted to humans. Rabies is usually transmitted by wild animals such as foxes, raccoons, skunks or bats, but infected cats and dogs can spread the disease as well. The virus is in the saliva of the infected animal. When an animal is bitten by an infected animal, the virus is deposited into a muscle or mucus membrane. The incubation period varies from two weeks to almost three months and in some cases longer, though that is rare.

Once in the body, the infection travels to the brain via the nerves and spinal cord. In most animals, the first sign of the disease is a change in behavior. Of course, the first sign of any sickness can be a change in behavior. Usually, a dog will start to get aggressive. As the virus runs its course, he may start salivating and drooling a lot and will have trouble swallowing. Next, paralysis or convulsions may occur, which may be followed by death. Don't take a chance with a disease like this: keep those rabies vaccinations up to date. When your veterinarian administers a rabies vaccine, you will get a dated tag and a certificate. Put the tag on Willy's collar. It will remind you of when the next shot is due. Usually, a puppy gets its first shot at five or six months, another a year later, and then every two years thereafter.

Internal Parasites

Internal parasites can cause a variety of problems. Many types are passed along through feces. At the park, for instance, if Willy sniffs at the feces of another dog that was in the park earlier, he can get worms. Some eggs live in the ground and can be absorbed through your dog's footpads. Humans can absorb worms through their feet or hands when walking or playing in infected soil.

The day you take your Lab for his yearly checkup, bring along a stool sample. Your veterinarian or a veterinary technician will look at the stool under a microscope. If eggs or the larvae of worms are present, he or she will identify them and prescribe the proper anthelmintic (worm medicine). *Remember, anthelmintics are poisons specifically formulated to kill one internal parasite or another and must be given carefully, according to directions.*

Following is a discussion of several types of worms and their mode of transmission.

Tapeworms: These worms are quite easy to see. You will notice what looks like moving grains of rice on your dog's stool after he defecates. You may find them around your dog's rectal area, on his hind legs and on his bedding. Dogs get tapeworm by ingesting fleas, which are the intermediate hosts. If Willy has had fleas recently, he will undoubtedly swallow some in his effort to rid himself of them. Chances are, he'll contract tapeworm as well. Usually, one worming is all that's necessary, but if you have another round of fleas, you will have to worm again. Tapeworms survive by attaching themselves to the wall of the intestines and absorbing nutrients. They are not the most serious or devastating intestinal parasites, but

These specks in your dog's fur mean he has fleas.

they can be debilitating. It is prudent to do a tape-worming after flea season.

Roundworms: Roundworms are probably the most common of the internal parasites, especially in puppies. They can be passed to the pups by the mother in utero. I routinely worm litters of pups (carefully) for roundworms and worm again fourteen days later. Then I have a fecal exam done to make sure the pups are clear. Older pups and adults pick up roundworms by sniffing feces of infected dogs. Female roundworms can lay thousands of eggs a day that are excreted with the feces. A heavy infestation can be serious, but regular stool checks for a new puppy and yearly checks for adult dogs should keep the problem in check.

Cleaning your yard every day is important for controlling all worms. Most important, keep Willy away from the feces of other dogs at curbside, in the park or on

The flea is a die-hard pest.

the beach. If he has round-worms and is treated, make sure you pick up and dispose of the feces immediately. Mature roundworms that are passed look somewhat like strands of spaghetti and can be eight to ten inches long. Pups that suffer from roundworm usually have pot bellies, a thin appearance and coats lacking a healthy shine or luster. Roundworms are actually more serious in humans than in canines, and you want to protect the health of your family as well as that of your pet. Your veterinarian may prescribe Panacure and Nemex to get rid of roundworms.

Hookworms: Signs of hookworm include bloody diarrhea or a somewhat slimy bloody stool. Hookworm eggs are passed in the feces like roundworms. They are very hardy and can live in sand or soil after the feces have been removed. The eggs hatch in the ground, and the larvae then enter a human or canine through the skin. After they burrow through the skin, the larvae migrate to the intestinal tract. Once attached to the intestinal wall, the worms suck the blood. When they leave one site for another, the first site bleeds, which causes the bloody stool.

Hookworms are hard to get rid of because once the worms are in your yard, they can survive a long time. Again, good sanitation is most important. Spray dog runs with bleach each time you clean and hose them. Spray the spots where dogs defecate with a bleach and water mixture. Also, be careful where you walk barefoot, in parks, at beaches or in your own yard.

Whipworms: These worms also feed on blood and live in the large intestine. As with some other internal parasites, whipworm eggs are shed in the stool and can also live in soil. Humans too can pick up whipworm from the soil, so it's a good idea to wear protective gloves when gardening.

Mature whips are about two to three inches long. They are somewhat thinner at one end than the other and not much thicker than a thread. They are shaped like a whip, hence, the name. Labs with bad infestations of whipworm can look thin and debilitated. Their coats will lack luster. They can also suffer from bloody diarrhea. Whipworms are not as easy to find as some other internal parasites because the eggs are not shed in the stool every day. You may take a stool sample to your veterinarian and have the sample checked. If you suspect whipworm, you should do stool checks four or five days in a row. Checks and treatment should be repeated.

Heartworm: Certain areas of the country suffer from heartworm more than others. It is transmitted by mosquitoes and because warmer climates have longer mosquito seasons, they experience more heartworm infestations. Detection takes about six months from the time a Lab is bitten until mature heartworms are found in the heart. Female heartworms give birth to live

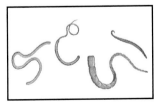

Common internal parasites (l-r): roundworm, whipworm, tapeworm and hookworm.

young called *microfilaria*. These microfilaria are picked up by the secondary host (the mosquito). When it bites an infected dog, the mosquito picks up some of the microfilaria. The mosquito then bites another dog, infecting it with the microfilaria, which then develops into mature heartworms, and the cycle continues ad infinitum.

We do have effective preventives for heartworm in pill form, which can be given daily or monthly. Before administering one, have your dog tested to make sure he isn't already infected with *microfilaria*. If he is and you unknowingly administer the preventive, he could die. Dogs that are infected can be treated, but the treatment is somewhat dangerous, and some dogs don't survive the treatment. Drugs that contain arsenic are administered to kill the adult worms. The dog has to be strong enough to withstand the treatment. His system must absorb the dead worms and then the microfilaria in the bloodstream must also be killed so that the cycle is broken. I've known several Labs that survived the treatment—they are troopers!

Use tweezers to remove ticks from your dog.

Protozoa

There are a few protozoan diseases that affect Labradors. A protozoan is a one-celled animal. Infestations occur when tiny cysts are ingested from contaminated feces. As distasteful as the thought may be, both puppies and dogs may, from time to time, eat feces. The cysts get into the lining of the bowel, where they mature.

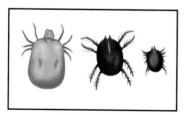

Three types of ticks (l-r): the wood tick, brown dog tick and deer tick.

Coccidioses or coccidia: Infestations of this protozoan are fairly common. Once in a breeder's kennel, no matter how often the premises are cleaned and disinfected, the problem will be chronic. Adult females become carriers, and their litters will be born with it. Luckily, it's easily detected through a fecal exam and easily treated with a product called Albon, an intestinal antibiotic. One of the first signs is usually a mucus-like diarrhea. Sometimes, you'll see a bit of blood. Puppies can also have runny eyes, noses or coughs. Coccidiosis is more commonly seen in puppies, but adults can have it or be carriers. Dogs can reinfect themselves by touching their own feces or the infected feces of other dogs. So once again, good sanitation is the key to control. It's important for large kennels not to keep dogs in overcrowded or cold, damp conditions.

Giardia: We find giardia in several areas of the country. It's quite common in wild animals. Willy may come upon contaminated feces in the woods or drink water from a contaminated puddle. Again, diarrhea is usually the first symptom. If you and your dog have been in the woods hiking and exploring or Willy has traveled to another part of the country where he has been romping through the woods, be on the lookout for diarrhea. Be sure to tell your veterinarian where your dog has been because it will help in the diagnosis. Giardia is usually successfully treated with Flagyl.

Orthopedic Problems

As with most large breeds, Labs have some orthopedic problems from time to time. Before getting into the specifics of these problems, I believe it's important for people to realize that in dogs as in humans things happen that are beyond our control. When people call me and inquire about buying a puppy, they often ask, "What guarantees do you give?" I reply, "I guarantee that you are getting a healthy puppy from two sound parents." I believe that is the best any breeder can do. Breeding dogs is not an exact science. There are some lines of Labradors that have a predisposition to certain orthopedic problems, but puppies that are overweight and do too much running too early in life can develop problems that would otherwise not surface.

Prudent breeders look at the big picture—not just the Orthopedic Foundation for Animals' (OFA) numbers or eye CERF's numbers or color or size. They do their best to select two individuals that complement each other structurally, and they are knowledgeable about the lines they are breeding. They have looked at the pedigrees and have learned as much as they can about what is behind each dog, and then they roll the dice! I have often heard dog owners malign a breeder because they bought a dog that developed a problem later in life. No one can predict the stress or trauma a dog may endure that will bring on problems. From time to time, children develop health problems, but we don't usually blame the parents or grandparents. If you have a problem, you seek what help is available for the specific problem and go on from there. We live in a time and country where we have some of the best medical technology available for people and their animals. For the animals sake, I'm not sure it's always a good thing, but that's another subject!

Canine Hip Dysplasia (CHD): CHD is a condition where the head of the femur does not properly fit into the hip socket. Dogs have left and right hips—think of each as a ball fitting into a socket that covers about three-fourths of the ball but allows the ball to rotate or move freely without friction. Strong tendons and muscles are needed for the hips to work correctly. If the acetabulum (socket) is too shallow or there is a flattening of the head of the femur (thighbone), the dog may experience pain. Every dog is different and has its own level of pain tolerance. Some Labs seem to cope with a set of hips that would leave another dog crying in pain. CHD

A FIRST-AID KIT

Keep a canine first-aid kit on hand for general care and emergencies. Check it periodically to make sure liquids haven't spilled or dried up, and replace medications and materials after they're used. Your kit should include:

Activated charcoal tablets

Adhesive tape
(1 and 2 inches wide)

Antibacterial ointment
(for skin and eyes)

Aspirin (buffered or enteric coated, *not* Ibuprofen)

Bandages: Gauze rolls (1 and 2 inches wide) and dressing pads

Cotton balls

Diarrhea medicine

Dosing syringe

Hydrogen peroxide (3%)

Petroleum jelly

Rectal thermometer

Rubber gloves

Rubbing alcohol

Scissors

Tourniquet

Towel

Tweezers

can cause several problems, ranging from a soreness that causes a mild lameness, irregularities in movement such as "bunny hopping" (picking up both legs at the same time when the dog tries to run) and trouble in getting up from a down position to crippling pain that keeps him from doing much of anything.

Experts are still debating about how much of CHD is inherited. It is thought to be a polygenic disorder (involving several genes). The part environmental factors play is still not known. I believe that a good diet and the right amount of exercise are critical during the developmental period of three months to one year, and they may contribute almost as much as genetics does to the reduction of CHD.

Several surgeries are available that may alleviate the pain of CHD. One is a Femoral Head Ostectomy (FHO), where the orthopedic surgeon removes the head of the femur. Hip replacements are another option. Pectineal myectomies and myotomies were done widely years ago but are not often done today, though I believe many were very successful and less costly.

The only way to diagnose CHD is to have your dog's hips radiographed or X-rayed. Preliminary X-rays can be done anytime. I usually do mine between eleven and fourteen months to get an idea of the quality. An X-ray for the OFA must be done at or after twenty-four months of age, when the dog is thought to be fully developed orthopedically. The OFA's panel of board-certified radiologists grade the hips and rate them excellent, good or fair if they conform; mild, moderate or severe if the dog is dysplastic. It is said that more good hips come from two excellent parents than from those who are only fair, although two moderate parents could produce puppies with good hips. Most experts agree that true hip dysplasia is bilateral (involving both hips). Often, cases that are unilateral (involving one hip) can be the result of a trauma.

Panosteitis: Pano is a disease that is hard to pin down. It's sometimes called "wandering lameness," because it can shift from limb to limb, or "growing pains." Pano is usually seen in Labradors from six to fourteen months of age. The lameness will seem to affect one leg and then another and can disappear after a few weeks or plague your dog for months. The good news is that dogs usually outgrow it. Dogs that are given pain medicine and then go out and overexercise will often take longer to recover, or worse, they may never totally recover. Pano has not been proven to be hereditary, but I have observed a prevalence of it in certain bloodlines.

Elbow Dysplasia: Elbow Dysplasia occurs when one of the elbow bones does not properly join the ulna. There can be loose fragments of bone that cause pain. Arthritis will usually follow at some point. The fragments may be surgically removed, alleviating the pain. I caution people not to go over the edge if their dog is diagnosed with this condition because I have seen the pain and lameness disappear without surgery. If your veterinarian recommends surgery, you might consider getting a second opinion, and let time and rest have a crack at it. Your dog may become asymptomatic.

Make a temporary splint by wrapping the leg in firm casing, then bandaging it.

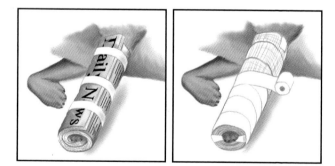

Osteochondritis Dissecans (OCD): This disease affects the larger, heavier-boned dog breeds. Some say that OCD is hereditary or that having cartilage that's easily damaged may be hereditary, but stress will aggravate the problem. OCD usually affects the shoulders or hock joints, though other joints can be affected. The condition is painful, and your dog will usually be lame. X-rays may show pieces of cartilage in the joint, and some veterinarians recommend surgery to remove these pieces. Again, I've known dogs to fully recover with rest and time. If surgery is recommended, I would think it over very carefully.

Giving Medications

At some time in your dog's life, he will probably need some kind of medication. Here are some tips for the administration of the medication.

Pills: Try sticking the pill to your damp thumb. Hold the upper jaw with your free hand and the lower jaw with the four free fingers on the hand with the pill. Aiming for the middle of the throat, as far back as possible, insert the pill and then quickly close the mouth. Hold it shut for a few seconds, and rub the throat to make your dog swallow. Another way is to disguise the pill in something your dog likes, such as cream cheese, chicken, butter or another type of cheese, and just hand it to him. Never put medication in your dog's food and assume he has swallowed it. Even if the bowl is empty, he may have taken the pill and spit it out.

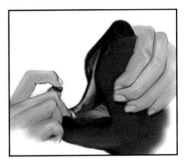

To give a pill, open the mouth wide, then drop it in the back of the throat.

Liquid medication: The easiest way to give a liquid medication is to measure it in a syringe (without a needle) or turkey baster and shoot it into your dog's mouth. I open the dog's mouth and aim for the side of the mouth or on the side under the tongue. You must be careful not to pour it down the dog's throat in such a way that he may inhale it rather than swallow it.

Ointment: Apply an ointment topically as you would to a human cut or abrasion. If your dog has a puncture wound, use something in a tube with an applicator that you can actually stick right into the wound and fill it from the inside out with the ointment. You want these wounds to heal from the inside out. Wipe the tube or applicator with an alcohol wipe when you're done.

Ear Medication: Liquid or ointment can go right down the ear canal. You don't want to just dab it around the surface; it needs to get down into the ear to do any good. Again, wipe the tube clean with an alcohol wipe.

Eye Medication: Putting ointment or other medication in your dog's eye is unlikely to be a fun experience for either of you, but a few simple guidelines should help you accomplish it with a minimum of discomfort and trauma. When applying ointment, assume a comfortable position. Sit on a chair with your dog's head on your lap, or sit on the floor next to your dog. If an extra pair of hands are available, ask someone to help hold the dog. Gently pull the lower eyelid down and squeeze the ointment out along the length of the lid. Try not to touch the tip of the tube to the dog's eye. Close the lid and gently rub the eye to distribute the medication through the eye. Reward your dog for his cooperation with a treat, which may also distract him from running to the living room rug and rubbing the medication out of his eye and all over the rug.

Eyedrops can be applied by gently pulling both the upper and lower lids open with your thumb and index

fingers and placing a few drops directly on the surface of the eyeball or under the lid. Again, be careful not to touch the tip of the dispenser to the surface of the eye. With a little practice, you should soon feel comfortable in dispensing needed medication easily.

Stitches and Wounds: Sometimes, Labs will incessantly bite or lick a healing wound. If this is the case and he is about to pull the stitches out or is keeping the wound from healing, your veterinarian may give you a large plastic collar called an Elizabethan collar. Your dog will have his head in the middle of this large cone-shaped collar (about two feet in diameter) and will not be able to get at the wound.

Plenty of exercise is important to ensure your dog's good health.

Other Concerns

Allergies: Labrador Retrievers can have allergic reactions to spider bites, bee stings or other insect bites. The affected area will usually swell. You should call your veterinarian, who may instruct you to give an antihistamine. You can also make a paste of water and baking soda, and apply it to the sting or bite to relieve the itching or burning.

Snakebite: If Willy is bitten by a snake, immobilize him to keep the venom from spreading through his system. You may need to muzzle him. If the bite is on a leg, restrict the flow further with a tourniquet (be careful to loosen it periodically). Get to a veterinarian as soon as possible. Try to identify the snake or at least be able to describe it to your veterinarian. You might be brave enough to kill the snake and take it with you to the veterinarian for identification. Identification helps in choosing the antivenom.

Applying abdominal thrusts can save a choking dog.

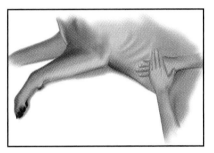

Choking: Labs love to carry things of all sizes. If something gets caught in Willy's throat and he is gagging, drooling and pawing at his mouth, get to your veterinarian as soon as possible. If it's something sharp, like a bone or stick, you may do damage by pulling it out. If it's something you can see and pull out, fine. You can use your fingers or a pair of pliers, tweezers or a hemostat. If you can't see the object, get someone to drive you to the veterinarian immediately. You can try a canine Heimlich maneuver to dislodge the object, but do this on your way to the veterinarian.

Car Accident: If Willy is hit by a car or other motor vehicle, he may have a broken limb or internal injuries, and moving him may cause further injury. Get a piece of plywood or something to use as a stretcher. If possible, summon help. Cover your dog with a blanket: he may be in shock. Secure him to the board, and get him to the veterinarian.

Porcupine Quills: Do not pull the quills out with your bare hands. Seek veterinary care, and have them removed while Willy is under sedation. If you are out in the woods and must deal with it yourself, try to cut the quills down to about an inch or so, and then pull them straight out with pliers.

Ripped or Torn Nails: A torn dewclaw can be very painful and will require a trip to your veterinarian. He or she will probably take it off completely. If one of the other nails gets caught and is torn, leaving the quick exposed, you need to go to your veterinarian. Your dog may need antibiotics to prevent infection. Keep the nail clean and pour hydrogen peroxide over it several times a day. If you are clipping the nails and cut a quick, there is a product called Quick Stop that comes in handy. It's a powder that you pack on the nail to stop the bleeding. If you don't have any, run the nail across a bar of soap: The soap will act as a stopper.

Poisoning: Depending on the poison, there may be different or multiple symptoms. Call your veterinarian immediately if you see any of the following alone or together: vomiting, diarrhea, drooling, labored breathing, seizures or convulsions, fever, chills or paralysis. If

Some of the many household substances harmful to your dog.

you know what the dog has gotten into, you can call Poison Control. They may be able to help. Though we try to keep obvious poisons out of reach, there may be plants indigenous to your area that are poisonous. If Willy has been out in the road or in a parking lot, he may have encountered a puddle of antifreeze, which is almost always fatal.

Lick Sores: These sores are usually a sign of boredom. A dog can give undivided attention to one spot, usually just above the top of the front paw, and keep at it until it's raw and bleeding. Try a change of scenery and increasing your dog's activity level. This is a behavioral problem and can be ongoing once it starts. Some products are available to keep your dog from attacking a sore. They usually contain a harmless ingredient with an unappealing taste, like Bitter Apple, but you can only use so much of this kind of thing; it's really more of a stopgap measure, not a cure. Changing Willy's scenery or lifestyle is the real answer. A dog that has time to lick incessantly is probably spending too much time alone with nothing better to do.

Hot Spots: These spots can be the result of fleas, other insect bites or an allergy. You see more hot spots in spring and summer. If your dog is swimming and lying around in the sand and dirt with a wet undercoat, there's a hot spot waiting to happen. Typically, the initial irritant makes the dog start to scratch or bite at the spot; hair loss will result, and as the dog keeps licking and scratching the irritated area, he may be left with large, oozing raw spots. Bacterial in nature, they can cause infection, requiring additional treatment.

Hot spots can be treated with antibacterial cleansers and a combination of antibiotics and steroids. If your dog seems to be in pain or if the spot seems infected, has a foul odor or is pussy, treatment is necessary. It's usually best to clip the hair (electric clippers work best) around the spot to let the sun and air get at it. If the spot is infected, you may need to first treat it with a topical antibiotic, but once the infection is gone you should try to dry up the spot.

An Elizabethan collar keeps your dog from licking a fresh wound.

Mange: Mange is caused by mites. It's an annoying problem that must be treated by your veterinarian. There are two types of mange: sarcoptic and demodectic. With sarcoptic (*sarcoptes scabiei var canis*, or scabies), the dog is usually extremely itchy and can have it from head to toe. Your veterinarian will need to do a skin scraping to identify the mites. The dog may need to have his hair shaved and be bathed repeatedly in an acaricide (shampoo or combination of chemical shampoos containing something like lindane, rotenone or malithion) to kill the mites. Treatment is usually successful. Sarcoptic mange is transmitted by direct contact and is the more contagious of the two types.

The second type, demodectic (*demonex canis*), is harder to get rid of than sarcoptic. There are two different forms of the demodectic: localized and generalized. These mites can travel from one dog or animal to another. Nursing puppies can get it from their mother if she is infested. It is a bit harder to scrape for demodectic mange because the mites may have to be squeezed out of a hair follicle and then be scraped. Your dog may have small hairless patches and rings around the eyes, or the whole body can be affected. The generalized type can be severe and almost impossible to get rid of and can involve the immune system. Antibiotics may be needed to fight secondary or bacterial infections. Complications can lead to death.

There are pesticides made to kill just about every pest alive, but remember, chemical warfare can become a vicious cycle. Before you resort to poisons, try some of the products that use natural oils such as pennyroyal or eucalyptus. Some of the citrus and oil combinations work well, too.

ADVANTAGES OF SPAY/NEUTER

The greatest advantage of spaying (for females) or neutering (for males) your dog is that you are guaranteed your dog will not produce puppies. There are too many puppies already available for too few homes. There are other advantages as well.

ADVANTAGES OF SPAYING

No messy heats.

No "suitors" howling at your windows or waiting in your yard.

Decreased incidences of pyometra (disease of the uterus) and breast cancer.

ADVANTAGES OF NEUTERING

Lessens male aggressive and territorial behaviors, but doesn't affect the dog's personality. Behaviors are often owner-induced, so neutering is not the only answer, but it is a good start.

Prevents the need to roam in search of bitches in season.

Decreased incidences of urogenital diseases.

Spaying and Neutering

There are far too many Labradors having puppies and siring litters that should never have been born. The AKC registers more Labradors yearly than any other breed, making them the most popular breed in the country. Also, more than any other breed, Labs and Lab mixes are found in pounds and shelters around the country. It's heartbreaking to see this fate happening to this wonderful breed.

There is no sense in adding to an already flooded market. There are plenty of puppies to be found advertised in the paper or in a pet store. Don't be part of the problem! Spaying and neutering are part of responsible ownership. Bitches that are not bred but come into heat every six months have a greater risk of uterine cancers and mammary tumors. Males that are not used for breeding and are not altered run a greater risk of having testicular cancer and prostate problems. Spay and neuter them if you love them and want what's best for the breed!

A Summer Concern

You should *never* leave any animal in a car in hot weather without proper ventilation, shade and water. When it's eighty-five degrees outside, it's much hotter in your car. Even with the windows slightly open, the temperature can reach 102 degrees in about ten minutes. In thirty minutes, it can be 120 degrees. Your dog could succumb to the heat and die while you're shopping in an air-conditioned mall. On extremely hot days, Willy will be happier at home. Even if he gets bored, he'll still be alive. Similarly, use caution in extremely cold weather to avoid exposure.

You are primarily responsible for your dog's health. You can help ensure a longer life of good quality by practicing good preventive care, seeing to it that your dog receives the proper diet, exercise and quality veterinary care he deserves.

First Aid

Although first aid is not a substitute for professional care, it can help save your dog's life.

To Stop Bleeding

Bleeding from a severe cut or wound must be stopped right away. There are two basic techniques: direct pressure and the tourniquet.

Try to control bleeding first by using direct pressure. Ask someone to hold the injured Labrador Retriever and place several pads of sterile gauze over the wound. Press. Do not wipe the wound or apply any cleansers or ointments. Apply firm, even pressure. If blood soaks through the pad, do not remove it as this could disrupt clotting. Simply place another pad on top and continue to apply pressure.

If bleeding on a leg or the tail does not stop by applying pressure, try using a tourniquet. Use this only as a last resort. A tourniquet that is left on too long can result in limb loss. To apply a tourniquet, do the following:

1. Wrap the limb or tail with one-inch gauze or a wide piece of cloth slightly above the wound and tie a half knot. Do not use a narrow band, rope or wire.
2. Place a pencil or stick on top and finish the knot.
3. Twist the pencil slowly until the bleeding stops. Fasten in place with tape.
4. Cover the wound with sterile gauze.
5. Once the tourniquet is on, take your dog to your veterinarian right away.

If your dog is bleeding from her mouth or anus, or vomits or defecates blood, she may be suffering from internal injuries. Do not attempt to stop bleeding. Call the veterinarian right away for emergency treatment.

CPR

Cardiopulmonary resuscitation, commonly called CPR, is a life-saving technique that provides artificial breathing and heart contractions for an unconscious animal whose heart and breathing have stopped. CPR combines artificial breathing with heart massage. Artificial respiration alone can be used for animals suffering respiratory distress—not combined with cardiac arrest—to aid breathing.

Dogs can suffer respiratory and cardiac failure for many reasons, including being hit by a car, poisoning or electrical shock. Respiratory distress is caused by many conditions, including a foreign object in the nasal passages, chest wounds or tearing of the diaphragm.

Do not attempt to perform CPR on a dog who has a heartbeat or perform artificial respiration on a conscious dog, unless his breathing is extremely shallow. In these instances, the life-saving techniques can harm an animal.

Artificial respiration: There are two methods of artificial respiration: *chest compression* and *mouth-to-nose*. Chest compression works by applying force to the chest wall, which pushes air out and allows the natural recoil of the chest to draw air in. It is the easiest to perform. Mouth-to-nose is forced respiration. It is used when the compression technique fails or when the chest is punctured.

To perform artificial respiration/chest compression:

1. Lay your lab on his right side and remove collar and harness.

2. Open your lab's mouth and check for possible obstructions.

3. Place both hands on the chest and press down sharply. Release quickly. If done properly, air should move in and out. If not, perform mouth-to-nose respiration.

4. Continue until your dog breathes on his own or as long as the heart beats.

To perform artificial respiration/mouth-to-nose:

1. Lay your lab on his right side and remove collar and harness.

2. Open your lab's mouth and check for possible obstructions.

3. Pull the tongue forward and close the mouth.

4. Place your mouth over your dog's nose and blow in steadily for three seconds. The chest will expand. Release for exhale.

5. Continue until your dog breathes on his own or as long as the heart beats.

Heart massage: Heart massage is used when there is no pulse, which often follows a cessation of breathing. To perform:

1. Feel for pulse or heartbeat.

2. Open your dog's mouth and check for possible obstructions.

3. Lay your dog on her right side and remove collar and harness.

4. Place your thumb on one side of the sternum and fingers on the other side just below the elbows. For large dogs, place the heel of your hand on rib cage behind the elbow, which is directly over the heart.

5. With hands in this position, squeeze firmly to compress the chest. Do so five to six times. Wait five seconds to let the chest expand and repeat.

6. Continue until the heart beats on its own or until no pulse is felt for five minutes.

Combining heart massage and artificial respiration may require two people, one to massage and one to respirate. In an emergency situation where no help is available, after five cardiac massages perform one artificial (mouth-to-nose) respiration without breaking the rhythm of the massages.

Your Happy, Healthy Pet

Your Dog's Name _____

Name on Your Dog's Pedigree (if your dog has one) _____

_____

Where Your Dog Came From _____

_____

Your Dog's Birthday _____

Your Dog's Veterinarian

    Name _____

    Address _____

    Phone Number_____

    Emergency Number_____

Your Dog's Health

    Vaccines

    type _____ date given _____

    type _____ date given _____

    type _____ date given _____

    type _____ date given _____

    Heartworm

    date tested _____ type used_____ start date _____

Your Dog's License Number_____

Groomer's Name and Number _____

Dogsitter/Walker's Name and Number_____

Awards Your Dog Has Won

    Award _____ date earned _____

    Award _____ date earned _____

part three

Enjoying
your
Dog

8

Basic
Training

by Ian Dunbar, Ph.D., MRCVS

Training is the jewel in the crown—the most important aspect of doggy husbandry. There is no more important variable influencing dog behavior and temperament than the dog's education: A well-trained, well-behaved and good-natured puppydog is always a joy to live with, but an untrained and uncivilized dog can be a perpetual nightmare. Moreover, deny the dog an education and it will not have the opportunity to fulfill its own canine potential; neither will it have the ability to communicate effectively with its human companions.

Luckily, modern psychological training methods are easy, efficient and effective and, above all, considerably dog-friendly and user-friendly. Doggy education is as simple as it is enjoyable. But before

98

you can have a good time play-training with your new dog, you have to learn what to do and how to do it. There is no bigger variable influencing the success of dog training than the *owner's* experience and expertise. *Before you embark on the dog's education, you must first educate yourself.*

Basic Training for Owners

Ideally, basic owner training should begin well *before* you select your dog. Find out all you can about your chosen breed first, then master rudimentary training and handling skills. If you already have your puppy/dog, owner training is a dire emergency—the clock is running! Especially for puppies, the first few weeks at home are the most important and influential days in the dog's life. Indeed, the cause of most adolescent and adult problems may be traced back to the initial days the pup explores his new home. This is the time to establish the *status quo*—to teach the puppy/dog how you would like him to behave and so prevent otherwise quite predictable problems.

In addition to consulting breeders and breed books such as this one (which understandably have a positive breed bias), seek out as many pet owners with your breed you can find. Good points are obvious. What you want to find out are the breed-specific *problems*, so you can nip them in the bud. In particular, you should talk to owners with *adolescent* dogs and make a list of all anticipated problems. Most important, *test drive* at least half a dozen adolescent and adult dogs of your breed yourself. An eight-week-old puppy is deceptively easy to handle, but she will acquire adult size, speed and strength in just four months, so you should learn now what to prepare for.

Puppy and pet dog training classes offer a convenient venue to locate pet owners and observe dogs in action. For a list of suitable trainers in your area, contact the Association of Pet Dog Trainers (see Chapter 13). You may also begin your basic owner training by observing other owners in class. Watch as many classes and test drive as many dogs as possible. Select an upbeat, dog-friendly, people-friendly, fun-and-games, puppydog pet training class to learn the ropes. Also, watch training videos and read training books (see Chapter 12). You must find out what to do and how to do it *before* you have to do it.

Principles of Training

Most people think training comprises teaching the dog to do things such as sit, speak and roll over, but even a four-week-old pup knows how to do these things already. Instead, the first step in training involves teaching the dog human words for each dog behavior and activity and for each aspect of the dog's environment. That way you, the owner, can more easily participate in the dog's domestic education by directing him to perform specific actions appropriately, that is, at the right time, in the right place, and so on. Training opens communication channels, enabling an educated dog to at least understand the owner's requests.

In addition to teaching a dog *what* we want her to do, it is also necessary to teach her *why* she should do what we ask. Indeed, 95 percent of training revolves around motivating the dog *to want to do* what we want. Dogs often understand what their owners want; they just don't see the point of doing it—especially when the owner's repetitively boring and seemingly senseless instructions are totally at odds with much more pressing and exciting doggy distractions. It is not so much the dog who is being stubborn or dominant; rather, it is the owner who has failed to acknowledge the dog's needs and feelings and to approach training from the dog's point of view.

The Meaning of Instructions

The secret to successful training is learning how to use training lures to predict or prompt specific behaviors—to coax the dog to do what you want *when* you want. Any highly valued object (such as a treat or toy) may be used as a lure, which the dog will follow with his eyes and nose. Moving the lure in specific ways entices the dog to move his nose, head and entire body in specific ways. In fact, by learning the art of manipulating various lures, it is possible to teach the dog to assume virtually any body position and perform any action. Once you have control over the expression of the dog's behaviors and can elicit any body position or behavior at will, you can easily teach the dog to perform on request.

Tell your dog what you want him to do, use a lure to entice him to respond correctly, then profusely praise

Teach your dog words for each activity he needs to know, like down.

and maybe reward him once he performs the desired action. For example, verbally request "Fido, sit!" while you move a squeaky toy upwards and backwards over the dog's muzzle (lure-movement and hand signal), smile knowingly as he looks up (to follow the lure) and sits down (as a result of canine anatomical engineering), then praise him to distraction ("Gooood Fido!"). Squeak the toy, offer a training treat and give your dog and yourself a pat on the back.

Being able to elicit desired responses over and over enables the owner to reward the dog over and over. Consequently, the dog begins to think training is fun. For example, the more the dog is rewarded for sitting, the more she enjoys sitting. Eventually the dog comes to realize that, whereas most sitting is appreciated, sitting immediately upon request usually prompts especially enthusiastic praise and a slew of high-level rewards. The dog begins to sit on cue much of the time, showing that she is starting to grasp the meaning of the owner's verbal request and hand signal.

Why Comply?

Most dogs enjoy initial lure/reward training and are only too happy to comply with their owners' wishes. Unfortunately, repetitive drilling without appreciative feedback tends to diminish the dog's enthusiasm until he eventually fails to see the point of complying anymore. Moreover, as the dog approaches adolescence he becomes more easily distracted as he develops other interests. Lengthy sessions with repetitive exercises tend to bore and demotivate both parties. If it's not fun, the owner doesn't do it and neither does the dog.

Integrate training into your dog's life: The greater number of training sessions each day and the *shorter* they are, the more willingly compliant your dog will become. Make sure to have a short (just a few seconds) training interlude before every enjoyable canine activity. For example, ask your dog to sit to greet people, to sit before you throw his Frisbee, and to sit for his supper. Really, sitting is no different from a canine "please." Also, include numerous short training interludes during every enjoyable canine pastime, for example, when playing with the dog or when he is running in the park. In this fashion, doggy distractions may be effectively converted into rewards for training. Just as all games have rules, fun becomes training . . . and training becomes fun.

Eventually, rewards actually become unnecessary to continue motivating your dog. If trained with consideration and kindness, performing the desired behaviors will become self-rewarding and, in a sense, your dog will motivate himself. Just as it is not necessary to reward a human companion during an enjoyable walk in the park, or following a game of tennis, it is hardly necessary to reward our best friend—the dog—for walking by our side or while playing fetch. Human company during enjoyable activities is reward enough for most dogs.

Even though your dog has become self-motivating, it's still good to praise and pet him a lot and offer rewards once in a while, especially for a good job well done. And if for no other reason, praising and rewarding others is good for the human heart.

To train your dog, you need gentle hands, a loving heart and a good attitude.

Punishment

Without a doubt, lure/reward training is by far the best way to teach: Entice your dog to do what you want and then reward him for doing so. Unfortunately, a human shortcoming is to take the good for granted and to moan and groan at the bad. Specifically, the dog's many good behaviors are ignored while the owner focuses on punishing the dog for making mistakes. In extreme cases, instruction is *limited* to punishing mistakes made by a trainee dog, child, employee or husband, even though it has been proven punishment training is notoriously inefficient and ineffective and is decidedly unfriendly and combative. It teaches the dog that training is a drag, almost as quickly as it teaches the dog to dislike his trainer. Why treat our best friends like our worst enemies?

Punishment training is also much more laborious and time consuming. Whereas it takes only a finite amount of time to teach a dog what to chew, for example, it takes much, much longer to punish the dog for each and every mistake. Remember, *there is only one right way!* So why not teach that right way from the outset?!

To make matters worse, punishment training causes severe lapses in the dog's reliability. Since it is obviously impossible to punish the dog each and every time she misbehaves, the dog quickly learns to distinguish between those times when she must comply (so as to avoid impending punishment) and those times when she need not comply, because punishment is impossible. Such times include when the dog is off leash and only six feet away, when the owner is otherwise engaged (talking to a friend, watching television, taking a shower, tending to the baby or chatting on the telephone), or when the dog is left at home alone.

Instances of misbehavior will be numerous when the owner is away, because even when the dog complied in the owner's looming presence, he did so unwillingly. The dog was forced to act against his will, rather than moulding his will to want to please. Hence, when the owner is absent, not only does the dog know he need not comply, he simply does not want to. Again, the trainee is not a stubborn vindictive beast, but rather the trainer has failed to teach.

Punishment training invariably creates unpredictable Jekyll and Hyde behavior.

Trainer's Tools

Many training books extol the virtues of a vast array of training paraphernalia and electronic and metallic gizmos, most of which are designed for canine restraint, correction and punishment, rather than for actual facilitation of doggy education. In reality, most effective training tools are not found in stores; they come from within ourselves. In addition to a willing dog, all you really need is a functional human brain, gentle hands, a loving heart and a good attitude.

In terms of equipment, all dogs do require a quality buckle collar to sport dog tags and to attach the leash (for safety and to comply with local leash laws). Hollow chewtoys (like Kongs or sterilized longbones) and a dog bed or collapsible crate are a must for housetraining. Three additional tools are required:

1. specific lures (training treats and toys) to predict and prompt specific desired behaviors;

2. rewards (praise, affection, training treats and toys) to reinforce for the dog what a lot of fun it all is; and

3. knowledge—how to convert the dog's favorite activities and games (potential distractions to training) into "life-rewards," which may be employed to facilitate training.

The most powerful of these is *knowledge*. Education is the key! Watch training classes, participate in training classes, watch videos, read books, enjoy playtraining with your dog, and then your dog will say "Please," and your dog will say "Thank you!"

Housetraining

If dogs were left to their own devices, certainly they would chew, dig and bark for entertainment and then no doubt highlight a few areas of their living space with sprinkles of urine, in much the same way we decorate by hanging pictures. Consequently, when we ask a dog to live with us, we must teach him *where* he may dig and perform his toilet duties, *what* he may chew and *when* he may bark. After all, when left at home alone for many hours, we cannot expect the dog to amuse himself by completing crosswords or watching the soaps on TV!

Also, it would be decidedly unfair to keep the house rules a secret from the dog, and then get angry and punish the poor critter for inevitably transgressing rules he did not even know existed. Remember, without adequate education and guidance, the dog will be forced to establish his own rules—doggy rules—that most probably will be at odds with the owner's view of domestic living.

Since most problems develop during the first few days the dog is at home, prospective dog owners must be certain they are quite clear about the principles of housetraining *before* they get a dog. Early misbehaviors quickly become established as the status quo—

becoming firmly entrenched as hard-to-break bad
habits, which set the precedent for years to come.
Make sure to teach your dog good habits right from
the start. Good habits are just as hard to break as bad
ones!

Ideally, when a new dog comes home, try to arrange
for someone to be present for as much as possible during the first few days (for adult dogs) or weeks for puppies. With only a little forethought, it is surprisingly
easy to find a puppy sitter, such as a retired person,
who would be willing to eat from your refrigerator and
watch your television while keeping an eye on the newcomer to encourage the dog to play with chewtoys and
to ensure he goes outside on a regular basis.

POTTY TRAINING

To teach the dog where to relieve himself:

1. never let him make a single mistake;

2. let him know where you want him to go; and

3. handsomely reward him for doing so:
   "GOOOOOOOD DOG!!!" liver treat, liver treat,
   liver treat!

PREVENTING MISTAKES

A single mistake is a training disaster, since it heralds
many more in future weeks. And each time the dog
soils the house, this further reinforces the dog's unfor-
tunate preference for an indoor, carpeted toilet. *Do not
let an unhousetrained dog have full run of the house if you
are away from home or cannot pay full attention.* Instead,
confine the dog to an area where elimination is appropriate, such as an outdoor run or, better still, a small,
comfortable indoor kennel with access to an outdoor
run. When confined in this manner, most dogs will naturally housetrain themselves.

If that's not possible, confine the dog to an area, such
as a utility room, kitchen, basement or garage, where

elimination may not be desired in the long run but as an interim measure it is certainly preferable to doing it all around the house. Use newspaper to cover the floor of the dog's day room. The newspaper may be used to soak up the urine and to wrap up and dispose of the feces. Once your dog develops a preferred spot for eliminating, it is only necessary to cover that part of the floor with newspaper. The smaller papered area may then be moved (only a little each day) towards the door to the outside. Thus the dog will develop the tendency to go to the door when he needs to relieve himself.

The first few weeks at home are the most important and influential in your dog's life.

Never confine an unhousetrained dog to a crate for long periods. Doing so would force the dog to soil the crate and ruin its usefulness as an aid for housetraining (see the following discussion).

TEACHING WHERE

In order to teach your dog where you would like her to do her business, you have to be there to direct the proceedings—an obvious, yet often neglected, fact of life. In order to be there to teach the dog *where* to go, you need to know *when* she needs to go. Indeed, the success of housetraining depends on the owner's ability to predict these times. Certainly, a regular feeding schedule will facilitate prediction somewhat, but there is

nothing like "loading the deck" and influencing the timing of the outcome yourself!

Whenever you are at home, make sure the dog is under constant supervision and/or confined to a small area. If already well trained, simply instruct the dog to lie down in his bed or basket. Alternatively, confine the dog to a crate (doggy den) or tie-down (a short, 18-inch lead that can be clipped to an eye hook in the baseboard). Short-term close confinement strongly inhibits urination and defecation, since the dog does not want to soil his sleeping area. Thus, when you release the puppydog each hour, he will definitely need to urinate immediately and defecate every third or fourth hour. Keep the dog confined to his doggy den and take him to his intended toilet area each hour, every hour, and on the hour.

When taking your dog outside, instruct him to sit quietly before opening the door—he will soon learn to sit by the door when he needs to go out!

TEACHING WHY

Being able to predict when the dog needs to go enables the owner to be on the spot to praise and reward the dog. Each hour, hurry the dog to the intended toilet area in the yard, issue the appropriate instruction ("Go pee!" or "Go poop!"), then give the dog three to four minutes to produce. Praise and offer a couple of training treats when successful. The treats are important because many people fail to praise their dogs with feeling . . . and housetraining is hardly the time for understatement. So either loosen up and enthusiastically praise that dog: "Wuzzzer-wuzzer-wuzzer, hoooser good wuffer den? Hoooo went pee for Daddy?" Or say "Good dog!" as best you can and offer the treats for effect.

Following elimination is an ideal time for a spot of playtraining in the yard or house. Also, an empty dog may be allowed greater freedom around the house for the next half hour or so, just as long as you keep an eye out to make sure he does not get into other kinds of mischief. If you are preoccupied and cannot pay full attention, confine the dog to his doggy den once more to enjoy a peaceful snooze or to play with his many chewtoys.

If your dog does not eliminate within the allotted time outside—no biggie! Back to his doggy den, and then try again after another hour.

As I own large dogs, I always feel more relaxed walking an empty dog, knowing that I will not need to finish our stroll weighted down with bags of feces! Beware of falling into the trap of walking the dog to get it to eliminate. The good ol' dog walk is such an enormous highlight in the dog's life that it represents the single biggest potential reward in domestic dogdom. However, when in a hurry, or during inclement weather, many owners abruptly terminate the walk the moment the dog has done its business. This, in effect, severely punishes the dog for doing the right thing, in the right place at the right time. Consequently, many dogs become strongly inhibited from eliminating outdoors because they know it will signal an abrupt end to an otherwise thoroughly enjoyable walk.

Instead, instruct the dog to relieve himself in the yard prior to going for a walk. If you follow the above instructions, most dogs soon learn to eliminate on cue. As soon as the dog eliminates, praise (and offer a treat or two)—"Good dog! Let's go walkies!" Use the walk as a reward for eliminating in the yard. If the dog does not go, put him back in his doggy den and think about a walk later on. You will find with a "No feces–no walk" policy, your dog will become one of the fastest defecators in the business.

If you do not have a back yard, instruct the dog to eliminate right outside your front door prior to the walk. Not only will this facilitate clean up and disposal of the feces in your own trash can but, also, the walk may again be used as a colossal reward.

CHEWING AND BARKING

Short-term close confinement also teaches the dog that occasional quiet moments are a reality of domestic living. Your puppydog is extremely impressionable during his first few weeks at home. Regular confinement at this time soon exerts a calming influence over the dog's personality. Remember, once the dog is housetrained and calmer, there will be a whole lifetime ahead for the dog to enjoy full run of the house and garden. On the other hand, by letting the newcomer have unrestricted access to the entire household and allowing him to run willy-nilly, he will most certainly develop a bunch of behavior problems in short order, no doubt necessitating confinement later in life. It would not be fair to remedially restrain and confine a dog you have trained, through neglect, to run free.

When confining the dog, make sure he always has an impressive array of suitable chewtoys. Kongs and sterilized longbones (both readily available from pet stores) make the best chewtoys, since they are hollow and may be stuffed with treats to heighten the dog's interest. For example, by stuffing the little hole at the top of a Kong with a small piece of freeze-dried liver, the dog will not want to leave it alone.

Remember, treats do not have to be junk food and they certainly should not represent extra calories. Rather, treats should be part of each dog's regular daily diet:

Make sure your puppy has suitable chewtoys.

Some food may be served in the dog's bowl for breakfast and dinner, some food may be used as training treats, and some food may be used for stuffing chewtoys. I regularly stuff my dogs' many Kongs with different shaped biscuits and kibble. The kibble seems to fall out fairly easily, as do the oval-shaped biscuits, thus rewarding the dog instantaneously for checking out the chewtoys. The bone-shaped biscuits fall out after a while, rewarding the dog for worrying at the chewtoy. But the triangular biscuits never come out. They remain inside the Kong as lures, maintaining the dog's fascination with its chewtoy. To further focus the dog's interest, I always make sure to flavor the triangular biscuits by rubbing them with a little cheese or freeze-dried liver.

If stuffed chewtoys are reserved especially for times the dog is confined, the puppy-dog will soon learn to enjoy quiet moments in her doggy den and she will quickly develop a chewtoy habit—a good habit! This is a simple *passive training* process; all the owner has to do is set up the situation and the dog all but trains herself—easy and effective. Even when the dog is given run of the house, her first inclination will be to indulge her rewarding chewtoy habit rather than destroying less-attractive household articles, such as curtains, carpets, chairs and compact disks. Similarly, a chewtoy chewer will be less inclined to scratch and chew herself excessively. Also, if the dog busies herself as a recreational chewer, she will be less inclined to develop into a recreational barker or digger when left at home alone.

Stuff a number of chewtoys whenever the dog is left confined and remove the extra-special-tasting treats when you return. Your dog will now amuse himself with his chewtoys before falling asleep and then resume playing with his chewtoys when he expects you to return. Since most owner-absent misbehavior happens right after you leave and right before your expected return, your puppydog will now be conveniently preoccupied with his chewtoys at these times.

Come and Sit

Most puppies will happily approach virtually anyone, whether called or not; that is, until they collide with

To teach come, call your dog, open your arms as a welcoming signal, wave a toy or a treat and praise for every step in your direction.

adolescence and develop other more important doggy interests, such as sniffing a multiplicity of exquisite odors on the grass. Your mission, Mr. and/or Ms. Owner, is to teach and reward the pup for coming reliably, willingly and happily when called—and you have just three months to get it done. Unless adequately reinforced, your puppy's tendency to approach people will self-destruct by adolescence.

Call your dog ("Fido, come!"), open your arms (and maybe squat down) as a welcoming signal, waggle a treat or toy as a lure, and reward the puppydog when he comes running. Do not wait to praise the dog until he reaches you—he may come 95 percent of the way and then run off after some distraction. Instead, praise the dog's *first* step towards you and continue praising enthusiastically for *every* step he takes in your direction.

When the rapidly approaching puppy dog is three lengths away from impact, instruct him to sit ("Fido, sit!") and hold the lure in front of you in an outstretched hand to prevent him from hitting you midchest and knocking you flat on your back! As Fido decelerates to nose the lure, move the treat upwards and backwards just over his muzzle with an upwards motion of your extended arm (palm-upwards). As the dog looks up to follow the lure, he will sit down (if he jumps up, you are holding the lure too high). Praise the dog for sitting. Move backwards and call him again. Repeat this many times over, always praising when Fido comes and sits; on occasion, reward him.

For the first couple of trials, use a training treat both as a lure to entice the dog to come and sit and as a reward for doing so. Thereafter, try to use different items as lures and rewards. For example, lure the dog with a Kong or Frisbee but reward her with a food treat. Or lure the dog with a food treat but pat her and throw a tennis ball as a reward. After just a few repetitions, dispense with the lures and rewards; the dog will begin to respond willingly to your verbal requests and hand signals just for the prospect of praise from your heart and affection from your hands.

Instruct every family member, friend and visitor how to get the dog to come and sit. Invite people over for a series of pooch parties; do not keep the pup a secret—let other people enjoy this puppy, and let the pup enjoy other people. Puppydog parties are not only fun, they easily attract a lot of people to help *you* train *your* dog. Unless you teach your dog *how* to meet people, that is, to sit for greetings, no doubt the dog will resort to jumping up. Then you and the visitors will get annoyed, and the dog will be punished. This is not fair. *Send out those invitations for puppy parties and teach your dog to be mannerly and socially acceptable.*

Even though your dog quickly masters obedient recalls in the house, his reliability may falter when playing in the back yard or local park. Ironically, it is *the owner* who has unintentionally trained the dog *not* to respond in these instances. By allowing the dog to play and run around and otherwise have a good time, but then to call the dog to put him on leash to take him home, the dog quickly learns playing is fun but training is a drag. Thus, playing in the park becomes a severe distraction, which works against training. Bad news!

Instead, whether playing with the dog off leash or on leash, request him to come at frequent intervals—say, every minute or so. On most occasions, praise and pet the dog for a few seconds while he is sitting, then tell him to go play again. For especially fast recalls, offer a couple of training treats and take the time to praise and pet the dog enthusiastically before releasing him. The dog will learn that coming when called is not necessarily the end of the play session, and neither is it the end of the world; rather, it signals an enjoyable, quality time-out with the owner before resuming play once more. In fact, playing in the park now becomes a very effective life-reward, which works to facilitate training by reinforcing each obedient and timely recall. Good news!

Sit, Down, Stand and Rollover

Teaching the dog a variety of body positions is easy for owner and dog, impressive for spectators and extremely useful for all. Using lure-reward techniques, it is possible to train several positions at once to verbal commands or hand signals (which impress the socks off onlookers).

Sit and ***down***—the two control commands—prevent or resolve nearly a hundred behavior problems. For example, if the dog happily and obediently sits or lies down when requested, he cannot jump on visitors, dash out the front door, run around and chase its tail, pester other dogs, harass cats or annoy family, friends or strangers. Additionally, "sit" or "down" are better emergency commands for off-leash control.

It is easier to teach and maintain a reliable sit than maintain a reliable recall. *Sit* is the purest and simplest of commands—either the dog is sitting or he is not. If there is any change of circumstances or potential danger in the park, for example, simply instruct the dog to sit. If he sits, you have a number of options: allow the dog to resume playing when he is safe; walk up and put the dog on leash, or call the dog. The dog will be much more likely to come when called if he has already acknowledged his compliance by sitting. If the dog does not sit in the park—train him to!

Stand and ***rollover-stay*** are the two positions for examining the dog. Your veterinarian will love you to distraction if you take a little time to teach the dog to stand still and roll over and play possum. Also, your vet bills will be smaller. The rollover-stay is an especially useful command and is really just a variation of the down-stay: whereas the dog lies prone in the traditional down, she lies supine in the rollover-stay.

As with teaching come and sit, the training techniques to teach the dog to assume all other body positions on cue are user-friendly and dog-friendly. Simply give the appropriate request, lure the dog into the desired body position using a training treat or toy and then *praise* (and maybe reward) the dog as soon as he complies. Try not to touch the dog to get him to respond. If you teach the dog by guiding him into position, the dog will quickly learn that rump-pressure means sit, for example, but as yet you still have no control over your dog if he is just six feet away. It will still be necessary to teach the dog to sit on request. So do not make training a time-consuming two-step process; instead, teach the dog to sit to a verbal request or hand signal from the outset. Once the dog sits willingly when requested, by all means use your hands to pet the dog when he does so.

To teach *down* when the dog is already sitting, say "Fido, down!," hold the lure in one hand (palm down) and lower that hand to the floor between the dog's forepaws. As the dog lowers his head to follow the lure, slowly move the lure away from the dog just a fraction (in front of his paws). The dog will lie down as he stretches his nose forward to follow the lure. Praise the dog when he does so. If the dog stands up, you pulled the lure away too far and too quickly.

When teaching the dog to lie down from the standing position, say "down" and lower the lure to the floor as before. Once the dog has lowered his forequarters and assumed a play bow, gently and slowly move the lure *towards* the dog between his forelegs. Praise the dog as soon as his rear end plops down.

After just a couple of trials it will be possible to alternate sits and downs and have the dog energetically perform doggy push-ups. Praise the dog a lot, and after half a dozen or so push-ups reward the dog with a training treat or toy. You will notice the more energetically you move your arm—upwards (palm up) to get the dog to sit, and downwards (palm down) to get the dog to lie down—the more energetically the dog responds to your requests. Now try training the dog in silence and you will notice he has also learned to respond to hand signals. Yeah! Not too shabby for the first session.

To teach *stand* from the sitting position, say "Fido, stand," slowly move the lure half a dog-length away from the dog's nose, keeping it at nose level, and praise the dog as he stands to follow the lure. As soon

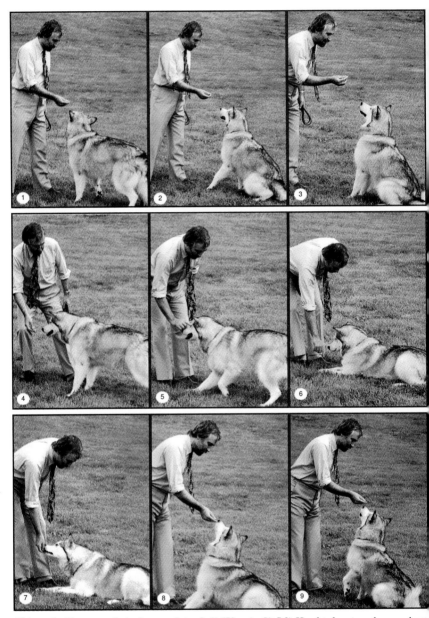

Using a food lure to teach sit, down and stand. 1) "Phoenix, Sit." 2) Hand palm upwards, move lure up and back over dog's muzzle. 3) "Good sit, Phoenix!" 4) "Phoenix, down." 5) Hand palm downwards, move lure down to lie between dog's forepaws. 6) "Phoenix, off. Good down, Phoenix!" 7) "Phoenix, sit!" 8) Palm upwards, move lure up and back, keeping it close to dog's muzzle. 9) "Good sit, Phoenix!"

0) "Phoenix, stand!" 11) Move lure away from dog at nose height, then lower it a tad. 12) "Phoenix, ff! Good stand, Phoenix!" 13) "Phoenix, down!" 14) Hand palm downwards, move lure down to lie tween dog's forepaws. 15) "Phoenix, off! Good down-stay, Phoenix!" 16) "Phoenix, stand!" 17) Move re away from dog's muzzle up to nose height. 18) "Phoenix, off! Good stand-stay, Phoenix. Now we'll ake the vet and groomer happy!"

as the dog stands, lower the lure to just beneath the dog's chin to entice him to look down; otherwise he will stand and then sit immediately. To prompt the dog to stand from the down position, move the lure half a dog-length upwards and away from the dog, holding the lure at standing nose height from the floor.

Teaching *rollover* is best started from the down position, with the dog lying on one side, or at least with both hind legs stretched out on the same side. Say "Fido, bang!" and move the lure backwards and alongside the dog's muzzle to its elbow (on the side of its outstretched hind legs). Once the dog looks to the side and backwards, very slowly move the lure upwards to the dog's shoulder and backbone. Tickling the dog in the goolies (groin area) often invokes a reflex-raising of the hind leg as an appeasement gesture, which facilitates the tendency to roll over. If you move the lure too quickly and the dog jumps into the standing position, have patience and start again. As soon as the dog rolls onto its back, keep the lure stationary and mesmerize the dog with a relaxing tummy rub.

To teach *rollover-stay* when the dog is standing or moving, say "Fido, bang!" and give the appropriate hand signal (with index finger pointed and thumb cocked in true Sam Spade fashion), then in one fluid movement lure him to first lie down and then rollover-stay as above.

Teaching the dog to *stay* in each of the above four positions becomes a piece of cake after first teaching the dog not to worry at the toy or treat training lure. This is best accomplished by hand feeding dinner kibble. Hold a piece of kibble firmly in your hand and softly instruct "Off!" Ignore any licking and slobbering *for however long the dog worries at the treat,* but say "Take it!" and offer the kibble *the instant* the dog breaks contact with his muzzle. Repeat this a few times, and then up the ante and insist the dog remove his muzzle for one whole second before offering the kibble. Then progressively refine your criteria and have the dog not touch your hand (or treat) for longer and longer periods on each trial, such as for two seconds, four seconds, then six, ten, fifteen, twenty, thirty seconds and so on. The dog soon learns: (1) worrying at the treat never gets results, whereas (2) noncontact is often rewarded after a variable time lapse.

Teaching *"Off!"* has many useful applications in its own right. Additionally, instructing the dog not to touch a training lure often produces spontaneous and magical stays. Request the dog to stand-stay, for example, and not to touch the lure. At first set your sights on a short two-second stay before rewarding the dog. (Remember, every long journey begins with a single step.) However, on subsequent trials, gradually and progressively increase the length of stay required to receive a reward. In no time at all your dog will stand calmly for a minute or so.

Relevancy Training

Once you have taught the dog what you expect her to do when requested to come, sit, lie down, stand, rollover and stay, the time is right to teach the dog *why* she should comply with your wishes. The secret is to have many (*many*) extremely short training interludes (two to five seconds each) at numerous (*numerous*) times during the course of the dog's day. Especially work with the dog immediately *before* the dog's good times and *during* the dog's good times. For example, ask your dog to sit and/or lie down each time before opening doors, serving meals, offering treats and tummy rubs; ask the dog to perform a few controlled doggy push-ups before letting her off-leash or throwing a tennis ball; and perhaps request the dog to sit-down-sit-stand-down-stand-rollover before inviting her to cuddle on the couch.

Similarly, request the dog to sit many times during play or on walks, and in no time at all the dog will be only too pleased to follow your instructions because he has learned that a compliant response heralds all sorts of goodies. Basically all you are trying to teach the dog is how to say please: "Please throw the tennis ball. Please may I snuggle on the couch."

Remember, whereas it is important to keep training interludes short, it is equally important to have many short sessions each and every day. The shortest (and most useful) session comprises asking the dog to sit and then go play during a play session. When trained this way, your dog will soon associate training with good times. In fact, the dog may be unable to distinguish between training and good times and, indeed, there should be no distinction. The warped concept that training involves forcing the dog to comply and/or dominating his will is totally at odds with the picture of a truly well-trained dog. In reality, enjoying a game of training with a dog is no different from enjoying a game of backgammon or tennis with a friend; and walking with a dog should be no different from strolling with buddies on the golf course.

Walk by Your Side

Many people attempt to teach a dog to heel by putting him on a leash and physically correcting the dog when he makes mistakes. There are a number of things seriously wrong with this approach, the first being that most people do not want precision heeling; rather, they simply want the dog to follow or walk by their side. Second, when physically restrained during "training," even though the dog may grudgingly mope by your side when "handcuffed" on leash, let's see what happens when he is off leash. History! The dog is in the next county because he never enjoyed walking with you on leash and you have no control over him off leash. So let's just teach the dog off leash from the outset to *want* to walk with us. Third, if the dog has not been trained to heel, it is a trifle hasty to think about punishing the poor dog for making mistakes and breaking heeling rules he didn't even know existed. This is simply not fair! Surely, if the dog had been adequately taught how to heel, he would seldom make mistakes and hence there would be no need to correct the dog. Remember, each mistake and each correction (punishment) advertise the trainer's inadequacy, not the dog's. The dog is not stubborn, he is not stupid and he is not bad. Even if he were, he would still require training, so let's train him properly.

Let's teach the dog to *enjoy* following us and to *want* to walk by our side offleash. Then it will be easier to teach high-precision off-leash heeling patterns if desired. After attaching the leash for safety on outdoor walks, but before going anywhere, it is necessary to teach the dog specifically not to pull. Now it will be much easier to teach on-leash walking and heeling because the dog already wants to walk with you, he is familiar with the desired walking and heeling positions and he knows not to pull.

FOLLOWING

Start by training your dog to follow you. Many puppies will follow if you simply walk away from them and maybe click your fingers or chuckle. Adult dogs may require additional enticement to stimulate them to follow, such as a training lure or, at the very least, a lively trainer. To teach the dog to follow: (1) keep walking and (2) walk away from the dog. If the dog attempts to lead or lag, change pace; slow down if the dog forges too far ahead, but speed up if he lags too far behind. Say "Steady!" or "Easy!" each time before you slow down and "Quickly!" or "Hustle!" each time before you speed up, and the dog will learn to change pace on cue. If the dog lags or leads too far, or if he wanders right or left, simply walk quickly in the opposite direction and maybe even run away from the dog and hide.

Practicing is a lot of fun; you can set up a course in your home, yard or park to do this. Indoors, entice the dog to follow upstairs, into a bedroom, into the bathroom, downstairs, around the living room couch, zigzagging between dining room chairs and into the kitchen for dinner. Outdoors, get the dog to follow around park benches, trees, shrubs and along walkways and lines in the grass. (For safety outdoors, it is advisable to attach a long line on the dog, but never exert corrective tension on the line.)

Remember, following has a lot to do with attitude—
your attitude! Most probably your dog will *not* want to
follow Mr. Grumpy Troll with the personality of wilted
lettuce. Lighten up—walk with a jaunty step, whistle a
happy tune, sing, skip and tell jokes to your dog and he
will be right there by your side.

BY YOUR SIDE

It is smart to train the dog to walk close on one side or
the other—either side will do, your choice. When walking, jogging or cycling, it is generally bad news to have
the dog suddenly cut in front of you. In fact, I train my
dogs to walk "By my side" and "Other side"—both very
useful instructions. It is possible to position the dog
fairly accurately by looking to the appropriate side and
clicking your fingers or slapping your thigh on that
side. A precise positioning may be attained by holding
a training lure, such as a chewtoy, tennis ball, or food
treat. Stop and stand still several times throughout the
walk, just as you would when window shopping or
meeting a friend. Use the lure to make sure the dog
slows down and stays close whenever you stop.

When teaching the dog to heel, we generally want
her to sit in heel position when we stop. Teach heel

*Using a toy to teach sit-heel-sit sequences: 1) "Phoenix, heel!" Standing still, move lure up and back
over dog's muzzle.... 2) To position dog sitting in heel position on your left side. 3) "Phoenix, heel!"
wagging lure in left hand. Change lure to right hand in preparation for sit signal.*

position at the standstill and the dog will learn that the default heel position is sitting by your side (left or right—your choice, unless you wish to compete in obedience trials, in which case the dog must heel on the left).

Several times a day, stand up and call your dog to come and sit in heel position—"Fido, heel!" For example, instruct the dog to come to heel each time there are commercials on TV, or each time you turn a page of a novel, and the dog will get it in a single evening.

Practice straight-line heeling and turns separately. With the dog sitting at heel, teach him to turn in place. After each quarter-turn, half-turn or full turn in place, lure the dog to sit at heel. Now it's time for short straight-line heeling sequences, no more than a few steps at a time. Always think of heeling in terms of Sit-Heel-Sit sequences—start and end with the dog in position and do your best to keep him there when moving. Progressively increase the number of steps in each sequence. When the dog remains close for 20 yards of straight-line heeling, it is time to add a few turns and then sign up for a happy-heeling obedience class to get some advice from the experts.

4) Use hand signal only to lure dog to sit as you stop. Eventually, dog will sit automatically at heel whenever you stop. 5) "Good dog!"

No Pulling on Leash

You can start teaching your dog not to pull on leash anywhere—in front of the television or outdoors—but regardless of location, you must not take a single step with tension in the leash. For a reason known only to dogs, even just a couple of paces of pulling on leash is intrinsically motivating and diabolically rewarding. Instead, attach the leash to the dog's collar, grasp the other end firmly with both hands held close to your chest, and stand still—do not budge an inch. Have somebody watch you with a stopwatch to time your progress, or else you will never believe this will work and so you will not even try the exercise, and your shoulder and the dog's neck will be traumatized for years to come.

Stand still and wait for the dog to stop pulling, and to sit and/or lie down. All dogs stop pulling and sit eventually. Most take only a couple of minutes; the all-time record is 22 $\frac{1}{5}$ minutes. Time how long it takes. Gently praise the dog when he stops pulling, and as soon as he sits, enthusiastically praise the dog and take just one step forwards, then immediately stand still. This single step usually demonstrates the ballistic reinforcing nature of pulling on leash; most dogs explode to the end of the leash, so be prepared for the strain. Stand firm and wait for the dog to sit again. Repeat this half a dozen times and you will probably notice a progressive reduction in the force of the dog's one-step explosions and a radical reduction in the time it takes for the dog to sit each time.

As the dog learns "Sit we go" and "Pull we stop," she will begin to walk forward calmly with each single step and automatically sit when you stop. Now try two steps before you stop. Wooooooo! Scary! When the dog has mastered two steps at a time, try for three. After each success, progressively increase the number of steps in the sequence: try four steps and then six, eight, ten and twenty steps before stopping. Congratulations! You are now walking the dog on leash.

Whenever walking with the dog (off leash or on leash), make sure you stop periodically to practice a few position commands and stays before instructing the dog to "Walk on!" (Remember, you want the dog to be compliant everywhere, not just in the kitchen when his dinner is at hand.) For example, stopping every 25 yards to briefly train the dog amounts to over 200 training interludes within a single three-mile stroll. And each training session is in a different location. You will not believe the improvement within just the first mile of the first walk.

To put it another way, integrating training into a walk offers 200 separate opportunities to use the continuance of the walk as a reward to reinforce the dog's education. Moreover, some training interludes may comprise continuing education for the dog's walking skills: Alternate short periods of the dog walking calmly by your side with periods when the dog is allowed to sniff and investigate the environment. Now sniffing odors on the grass and meeting other dogs become rewards which reinforce the dog's calm and mannerly demeanor. Good Lord! Whatever next? Many enjoyable walks together of course. Happy trails!

THE IMPORTANCE OF TRICKS

Nothing will improve a dog's quality of life better than having a few tricks under its belt. Teaching any trick expands the dog's vocabulary, which facilitates communication and improves the owner's control. Also, specific tricks help prevent and resolve specific behavior problems. For example, by teaching the dog to fetch his toys, the dog learns carrying a toy makes the owner happy and, therefore, will be more likely to chew his toy than other inappropriate items.

More important, teaching tricks prompts owners to lighten up and train with a sunny disposition. Really, tricks should be no different from any other behaviors we put on cue. But they are. When teaching tricks, owners have a much sweeter attitude, which in turn motivates the dog and improves her willingness to comply. The dog feels tricks are a blast, but formal commands are a drag. In fact, tricks are so enjoyable, they may be used as rewards in training by asking the dog to come, sit and down-stay and then rollover for a tummy rub. Go on, try it: Crack a smile and even giggle when the dog promptly and willingly lies down and stays.

Most important, performing tricks prompts onlookers to smile and gig-gle. Many people are scared of dogs, especially large ones. And noth-ing can be more off-putting for a dog than to be constantly confronted by strangers who don't like him because of his size or the way he looks. Uneasy people put the dog on edge, causing him to back off and bark, only frightening people all the more. And so a vicious circle develops, with the people's fear fueling the dog's fear *and vice versa.* Instead, tie a pink ribbon to your dog's collar and practice all sorts of tricks on walks and in the park, and you will be pleasantly amazed how it changes people's attitudes toward your friendly dog. The dog's reper-toire of tricks is limited only by the trainer's imagination. Below I have described three of my favorites:

SPEAK AND SHUSH

The training sequence involved in teaching a dog to bark on request is no different from that used when training any behavior on cue: request—lure—response—reward. As always, the secret of success lies in finding an effective lure. If the dog always barks at the doorbell, for example, say "Rover, speak!", have an accomplice ring the doorbell, then reward the dog for barking. After a few woofs, ask Rover to "Shush!", waggle a food treat under his nose (to entice him to sniff and thus to shush), praise him when quiet and eventually offer the treat as a reward. Alternate "Speak" and "Shush," progressively increasing the length of shush-time between each barking bout.

PLAYBOW

With the dog standing, say "Bow!" and lower the food lure (palm upwards) to rest between the dog's forepaws. Praise as the dog lowers

her forequarters and sternum to the ground (as when teaching the down), but then lure the dog to stand and offer the treat. On successive trials, gradually increase the length of time the dog is required to remain in the playbow posture in order to gain a food reward. If the dog's rear end collapses into a down, say nothing and offer no reward; simply start over.

BE A BEAR

With the dog sitting backed into a corner to prevent him from toppling over backwards, say "Be a Bear!" With bent paw and palm down, raise a lure upwards and backwards along the top of the dog's muzzle. Praise the dog when he sits up on his haunches and offer the treat as a reward. To prevent the dog from standing on his hind legs, keep the lure closer to the dog's muzzle. On each trial, progressively increase the length of time the dog is required to sit up to receive a food reward. Since lure/reward training is so easy, teach the dog to stand and walk on his hind legs as well!

Teaching "Be a Bear"

chapter 9

Getting
Active
with your Dog

by Bardi McLennan

Once you and your dog have graduated from basic obedience training and are beginning to work together as a team, you can take part in the growing world of dog activities. There are so many fun things to do with your dog! Just remember, people and dogs don't always learn at the same pace, so don't be upset if you (or your dog) need more than two basic training courses before your team becomes operational. Even smart dogs don't go straight to college from kindergarten!

Just as there are events geared to certain types of dogs, so there are ones that are more appealing to certain types of people. In some activities, you give the commands and your dog does the work (upland game hunting is one example), while in others, such as agility, you'll both get a workout. You may want to aim for prestigious titles to add to your dog's name, or you may want nothing more than the sheer enjoyment of being around other people and their dogs. Passive or active, participation has its own rewards.

Consider your dog's physical capabilities when looking into any of the canine activities. It's easy to see that a Basset Hound is not built for the racetrack, nor would a Chihuahua be the breed of choice for pulling a sled.   A loyal dog will attempt almost anything you ask him to do, so it is up to you to know your

All dogs seem to love playing flyball.

dog's limitations. A dog must be physically sound in order to compete at any level in athletic activities, and being mentally sound is a definite plus. Advanced age, however, may not be a deterrent. Many dogs still hunt and herd at ten or twelve years of age. It's entirely possible for dogs to be "fit at 50." Take your dog for a checkup, explain to your vet the type of activity you have in mind and be guided by his or her findings.

You needn't be restricted to breed-specific sports if it's only fun you're after. Certain AKC activities are limited to designated breeds; however, as each new trial, test or sport has grown in popularity, so has the variety of breeds encouraged to participate at a fun level.

But don't shortchange your fun, or that of your dog, by thinking only of the basic function of her breed. Once a dog has learned how to learn, she can be taught to do just about anything as long as the size of the dog is right for the job and you both think it is fun and rewarding. In other words, you are a team.

To get involved in any of the activities detailed in this chapter, look for the names and addresses of the organizations that sponsor them in Chapter 13. You can also ask your breeder or a local dog trainer for contacts.

You can compete in obedience trials with a well trained dog.

Official American Kennel Club Activities

The following tests and trials are some of the events sanctioned by the AKC and sponsored by various dog clubs. Your dog's expertise will be rewarded with impressive titles. You can participate just for fun, or be competitive and go for those awards.

OBEDIENCE

Training classes begin with pups as young as three months of age in kindergarten puppy training, then advance to pre-novice (all exercises on lead) and go on to novice, which is where you'll start off-lead work. In obedience classes dogs learn to sit, stay, heel and come through a variety of exercises. Once you've got the basics down, you can enter obedience trials and work toward earning your dog's first degree, a C.D. (Companion Dog).

The next level is called "Open," in which jumps and retrieves perk up the dog's interest. Passing grades in competition at this level earn a C.D.X. (Companion Dog Excellent). Beyond that lies the goal of the most ambitious—Utility (U.D. and even U.D.X. or OTCh, an Obedience Champion).

AGILITY

All dogs can participate in the latest canine sport to have gained worldwide popularity for its fun and excitement, agility. It began in England as a canine version of horse show-jumping, but because dogs are more agile and able to perform on verbal commands, extra feats were added such as climbing, balancing and racing through tunnels or in and out of weave poles. Many of the obstacles (regulation or homemade) can be set up in your own backyard. If the agility bug bites, you could end up in international competition!

For starters, your dog should be obedience trained, even though, in the beginning, the lessons may all be taught on lead. Once the dog understands the commands (and you do, too), it's as easy as guiding the dog over a prescribed course, one obstacle at a time. In competition, the race is against the clock, so wear your running shoes! The dog starts with 200 points and the judge deducts for infractions and misadventures along the way.

All dogs seem to love agility and respond to it as if they were being turned loose in a playground paradise. Your dog's enthusiasm will be contagious; agility turns into great fun for dog and owner.

FIELD TRIALS AND HUNTING TESTS

There are field trials and hunting tests for the sporting breeds—retrievers, spaniels and pointing breeds, and for some hounds—Bassets, Beagles and Dachshunds. Field trials are competitive events that test a dog's ability to perform the functions for which she was bred. Hunting tests, which are open to retrievers,

---

TITLES AWARDED BY THE AKC

Conformation: Ch. (Champion)

Obedience: CD (Companion Dog); CDX (Companion Dog Excellent); UD (Utility Dog); UDX (Utility Dog Excellent); OTCh. (Obedience Trial Champion)

Field: JH (Junior Hunter); SH (Senior Hunter); MH (Master Hunter); AFCh. (Amateur Field Champion); FCh. (Field Champion)

Lure Coursing: JC (Junior Courser); SC (Senior Courser)

Herding: HT (Herding Tested); PT (Pre-Trial Tested); HS (Herding Started); HI (Herding Intermediate); HX (Herding Excellent); HCh. (Herding Champion)

Tracking: TD (Tracking Dog); TDX (Tracking Dog Excellent)

Agility: NAD (Novice Agility); OAD (Open Agility); ADX (Agility Excellent); MAX (Master Agility)

Earthdog Tests: JE (Junior Earthdog); SE (Senior Earthdog); ME (Master Earthdog)

Canine Good Citizen: CGC

Combination: DC (Dual Champion—Ch. and Fch.); TC (Triple Champion—Ch., Fch., and OTCh.)

spaniels and pointing breeds only, are noncompetitive and are a means of judging the dog's ability as well as that of the handler.

Hunting is a very large and complex part of canine sports, and if you own one of the breeds that hunts, the events are a great treat for your dog and you. He gets to do what he was bred for, and you get to work with him and watch him do it. You'll be proud of and amazed at what your dog can do.

Fortunately, the AKC publishes a series of booklets on these events, which outline the rules and regulations and include a glossary of the sometimes complicated terms. The AKC also publishes newsletters for field trialers and hunting test enthusiasts. The United Kennel Club (UKC) also has informative materials for the hunter and his dog.

Retrievers and other sporting breeds get to do what they're bred to in hunting tests.

HERDING TESTS AND TRIALS

Herding, like hunting, dates back to the first known uses man made of dogs. The interest in herding today is widespread, and if you own a herding breed, you can join in the activity. Herding dogs are tested for their natural skills to keep a flock of ducks, sheep or cattle together. If your dog shows potential, you can start at the testing level, where your dog can earn a title for showing an inherent herding ability. With training you can advance to the trial level, where your dog should be capable of controlling even difficult livestock in diverse situations.

LURE COURSING

The AKC Tests and Trials for Lure Coursing are open to traditional sighthounds—Greyhounds, Whippets,

Borzoi, Salukis, Afghan Hounds, Ibizan Hounds and Scottish Deerhounds—as well as to Basenjis and Rhodesian Ridgebacks. Hounds are judged on overall ability, follow, speed, agility and endurance. This is possibly the most exciting of the trials for spectators, because the speed and agility of the dogs is awesome to watch as they chase the lure (or "course") in heats of two or three dogs at a time.

TRACKING

Tracking is another activity in which almost any dog can compete because every dog that sniffs the ground when taken outdoors is, in fact, tracking. The hard part comes when the rules as to what, when and where the dog tracks are determined by a person, not the dog! Tracking tests cover a large area of fields, woods and roads. The tracks are laid hours before the dogs go to work on them, and include "tricks" like cross-tracks and sharp turns. If you're interested in search-and-rescue work, this is the place to start.

This tracking dog is hot on the trail.

EARTHDOG TESTS FOR SMALL TERRIERS AND DACHSHUNDS

These tests are open to Australian, Bedlington, Border, Cairn, Dandie Dinmont, Smooth and Wire Fox, Lakeland, Norfolk, Norwich, Scottish, Sealyham, Skye, Welsh and West Highland White Terriers as well as Dachshunds. The dogs need no prior training for this terrier sport. There is a qualifying test on the day of the event, so dog and handler learn the rules on the spot. These tests, or "digs," sometimes end with informal races in the late afternoon.

Here are some of the extracurricular obedience and racing activities that are not regulated by the AKC or UKC, but are generally run by clubs or a group of dog fanciers and are often open to all.

Canine Freestyle This activity is something new on the scene and is variously likened to dancing, dressage or ice skating. It is meant to show the athleticism of the dog, but also requires showmanship on the part of the dog's handler. If you and your dog like to ham it up for friends, you might want to look into freestyle.

Lure coursing lets sighthounds do what they do best—run!

Scent Hurdle Racing Scent hurdle racing is purely a fun activity sponsored by obedience clubs with members forming competing teams. The height of the hurdles is based on the size of the shortest dog on the team. On a signal, one team dog is released on each of two side-by-side courses and must clear every hurdle before picking up its own dumbbell from a platform and returning over the jumps to the handler. As each dog returns, the next on that team is sent. Of course, that is what the dogs are supposed to do. When the dogs improvise (going under or around the hurdles, stealing another dog's dumbbell, and so forth), it no doubt frustrates the handlers, but just adds to the fun for everyone else.

Flyball This type of racing is similar, but after negotiating the four hurdles, the dog comes to a flyball box, steps on a lever that releases a tennis ball into the air, catches the ball and returns over the hurdles to the starting point. This game also becomes extremely fun for spectators because the dogs sometimes cheat by catching a ball released by the dog in the next lane. Three titles can be earned—Flyball Dog (F.D.), Flyball Dog Excellent (F.D.X.) and Flyball Dog Champion (Fb.D.Ch.)—all awarded by the North American Flyball Association, Inc.

Dogsledding The name conjures up the Rocky Mountains or the frigid North, but you can find dogsled clubs in such unlikely spots as Maryland, North Carolina and Virginia! Dogsledding is primarily for the Nordic breeds such as the Alaskan Malamutes, Siberian Huskies and Samoyeds, but other breeds can try. There are some practical backyard applications to this sport, too. With parental supervision, almost any strong dog could pull a child's sled.

Coming over the A-frame on an agility course.

These are just some of the many recreational ways you can get to know and understand your multifaceted dog better and have fun doing it.

chapter 10

Your Dog
and your
Family

by Bardi McLennan

Adding a dog automatically increases your family by one, no matter whether you live alone in an apartment or are part of a mother, father and six kids household. The single-person family is fair game for numerous and varied canine misconceptions as to who is dog and who pays the bills, whereas a dog in a houseful of children will consider himself to be just one of the gang, littermates all. One dog and one child may give a dog reason to believe they are both kids or both dogs. Either interpretation requires parental supervision and sometimes speedy intervention.

As soon as one paw goes through the door into your home, Rufus (or Rufina) has to make many adjustments to become a part of your family. Your job is to make him fit in as painlessly as possible. An older dog may have some frame of reference from past experience, but to a 10-week-old puppy, everything is brand new: people, furniture, stairs, when and where people eat, sleep or watch TV, his own place and everyone else's space, smells, sounds, outdoors—everything!

Puppies, and newly acquired dogs of any age, do not need what we think of as "freedom." If you leave a new dog or puppy loose in the house, you will almost certainly return to chaotic destruction and the dog will forever after equate your homecoming with a time of punishment to be dreaded. It is unfair to give your dog what amounts to "freedom to get into trouble." Instead, confine him to a crate for brief periods of your absence (up to three or four hours) and, for the long haul, a workday for example, confine him to one untrashable area with his own toys, a bowl of water and a radio left on (low) in another room.

Lots of pets get along with each other just fine.

For the first few days, when not confined, put Rufus on a long leash tied to your wrist or waist. This umbilical cord method enables the dog to learn all about you from your body language and voice, and to learn by his own actions which things in the house are NO! and which ones are rewarded by "Good dog." Housetraining will be easier with the pup always by your side. Speaking of which, accidents do happen. That goal of "completely housetrained" takes up to a year, or the length of time it takes the pup to mature.

The All-Adult Family

Most dogs in an adults-only household today are likely to be latchkey pets, with no one home all day but the dog. When you return after a tough day on the job, the dog can and should be your relaxation therapy. But going home can instead be a daily frustration.

Separation anxiety is a very common problem for the dog in a working household. It may begin with whines and barks of loneliness, but it will soon escalate into a frenzied destruction derby. That is why it is so important to set aside the time to teach a dog to relax when left alone in his confined area and to understand that he can trust you to return.

Let the dog get used to your work schedule in easy stages. Confine him to one room and go in and out of that room over and over again. Be casual about it. No physical, voice or eye contact. When the pup no longer even notices your comings and goings, leave the house for varying lengths of time, returning to stay home for a few minutes and gradually increasing the time away. This training can take days, but the dog is learning that you haven't left him forever and that he can trust you.

Any time you leave the dog, but especially during this training period, be casual about your departure. No anxiety-building fond farewells. Just "Bye" and go! Remember the "Good dog" when you return to find everything more or less as you left it.

If things are a mess (or even a disaster) when you return, greet the dog, take him outside to eliminate, and then put him in his crate while you clean up. Rant and rave in the shower! *Do not* punish the dog. You were not there when it happened, and the rule is: Only punish as you catch the dog in the act of wrongdoing. Obviously, it makes sense to get your latchkey puppy when you'll have a week or two to spend on these training essentials.

Family weekend activities should include Rufus whenever possible. Depending on the pup's age, now is the time for a long walk in the park, playtime in the backyard, a hike in the woods. Socializing is as important as health care, good food and physical exercise, so visiting Aunt Emma or Uncle Harry and the next-door neighbor's dog or cat is essential to developing an outgoing, friendly temperament in your pet.

If you are a single adult, socializing Rufus at home and away will prevent him from becoming overly protective of you (or just overly attached) and will also prevent such behavioral problems as dominance or fear of strangers.

Babies

Whether already here or on the way, babies figure larger than life in the eyes of a dog. If the dog is there first, let him in on all your baby preparations in the house. When baby arrives, let Rufus sniff any item of clothing that has been on the baby before Junior comes home. Then let Mom greet the dog first before introducing the new family member. Hold the baby down for the dog to see and sniff, but make sure someone's holding the dog on lead in case of any sudden moves. Don't play keep-away or tease the dog with the baby, which only invites undesirable jumping up.

The dog and the baby are "family," and for starters can be treated almost as equals. Things rapidly change, however, especially when baby takes to creeping around on all fours on the dog's turf or, better yet, has yummy pudding all over her face and hands! That's when a lot of things in the dog's and baby's lives become more separate than equal.

Dogs are perfect confidants.

Toddlers make terrible dog owners, but if you can't avoid the combination, use patient discipline (that is, positive teaching rather than punishment), and use time-outs before you run out of patience.

A dog and a baby (or toddler, or an assertive young child) should never be left alone together. Take the dog with you or confine him. With a baby or youngsters in the house, you'll have plenty of use for that wonderful canine safety device called a crate!

Young Children

Any dog in a house with kids will behave pretty much as the kids do, good or bad. But even good dogs and good children can get into trouble when play becomes rowdy and active.

Teach children how to play nicely with a puppy.

Legs bobbing up and down, shrill voices screeching, a ball hurtling overhead, all add up to exuberant frustration for a dog who's just trying to be part of the gang. In a pack of puppies, any legs or toys being chased would be caught by a set of teeth, and all the pups involved would understand that is how the game is played. Kids do not understand this, nor do parents tolerate it. Bring Rufus indoors before you have reason to regret it. This is time-out, not a punishment.

You can explain the situation to the children and tell them they must play quieter games until the puppy learns not to grab them with his mouth. Unfortunately, you can't explain it that easily to the dog. With adult supervision, they will learn how to play together.

Young children love to tease. Sticking their faces or wiggling their hands or fingers in the dog's face is teasing. To another person it might be just annoying, but it is threatening to a dog. There's another difference: We can make the child stop by an explanation, but the only way a dog can stop it is with a warning growl and then with teeth. Teasing is the major cause of children being bitten by their pets. Treat it seriously.

Older Children

The best age for a child to get a first dog is between the ages of 8 and 12. That's when kids are able to accept some real responsibility for their pet. Even so, take the child's vow of "I will never *ever* forget to feed (brush, walk, etc.) the dog" for what it's worth: a child's good intention at that moment. Most kids today have extra lessons, soccer practice, Little League, ballet, and so forth piled on top of school schedules. There will be many times when Mom will have to come to the dog's rescue. "I walked the dog for you so you can set the table for me" is one way to get around a missed appointment without laying on blame or guilt.

Kids in this age group make excellent obedience trainers because they are into the teaching/learning process themselves and they lack the self-consciousness of adults. Attending a dog show is something the whole family can enjoy, and watching Junior Showmanship may catch the eye of the kids. Older children can begin to get involved in many of the recreational activities that were reviewed in the previous chapter. Some of the agility obstacles, for example, can be set up in the backyard as a family project (with an adult making sure all the equipment is safe and secure for the dog).

Older kids are also beginning to look to the future, and may envision themselves as veterinarians or trainers or show dog handlers or writers of the next Lassie best-seller. Dogs are perfect confidants for these dreams. They won't tell a soul.

Other Pets

Introduce all pets tactfully. In a dog/cat situation, hold the dog, not the cat. Let two dogs meet on neutral turf—a stroll in the park or a walk down the street—with both on loose leads to permit all the normal canine ways of saying hello, including routine sniffing, circling, more sniffing, and so on. Small creatures such as hamsters, chinchillas or mice must be kept safe from their natural predators (dogs and cats).

Festive Family Occasions

Parties are great for people, but not necessarily for puppies. Until all the guests have arrived, put the dog in his crate or in a room where he won't be disturbed. A socialized dog can join the fun later as long as he's not underfoot, annoying guests or into the hors d'oeuvres.

There are a few dangers to consider, too. Doors opening and closing can allow a puppy to slip out unnoticed in the confusion, and you'll be organizing a search party instead of playing host or hostess. Party food and buffet service are not for dogs. Let Rufus party in his crate with a nice big dog biscuit.

At Christmas time, not only are tree decorations dangerous and breakable (and perhaps family heirlooms), but extreme caution should be taken with the lights, cords and outlets for the tree lights and any other festive lighting. Occasionally a dog lifts a leg, ignoring the fact that the tree is indoors. To avoid this, use a canine repellent, made for gardens, on the tree. Or keep him out of the tree room unless supervised. And whatever you do, *don't* invite trouble by hanging his toys on the tree!

Car Travel

Before you plan a vacation by car or RV with Rufus, be sure he enjoys car travel. Nothing spoils a holiday quicker than a carsick dog! Work within the dog's comfort level. Get in the car with the dog in his crate or attached to a canine car safety belt and just sit there until he relaxes. That's all. Next time, get in the car, turn on the engine and go nowhere. Just sit. When that is okay, turn on the engine and go around the block. Now you can go for a ride and include a stop where you get out, leaving the dog for a minute or two.

On a warm day, always park in the shade and leave windows open several inches. And return quickly. It only takes 10 minutes for a car to become an overheated steel death trap.

Motel or Pet Motel?

Not all motels or hotels accept pets, but you have a much better choice today than even a few years ago. To find a dog-friendly lodging, look at *On the Road Again With Man's Best Friend*, a series of directories that detail bed and breakfasts, inns, family resorts and other hotels/motels. Some places require a refundable deposit to cover any damage incurred by the dog. More B&Bs accept pets now, but some restrict the size.

If taking Rufus with you is not feasible, check out boarding kennels in your area. Your veterinarian may offer this service, or recommend a kennel or two he or she is familiar with. Go see the facilities for yourself, ask about exercise, diet, housing, and so on. Or, if you'd rather have Rufus stay home, look into bonded petsitters, many of whom will also bring in the mail and water your plants.

Your Dog
and your
Community

by Bardi McLennan

Step outside your home with your dog and you are no longer just family, you are both part of your community. This is when the phrase "responsible pet ownership" takes on serious implications. For starters, it means you pick up after your dog—not just occasionally, but every time your dog eliminates away from home. That means you have joined the Plastic Baggy Brigade! You always have plastic sandwich bags in your pocket and several in the car. It means you teach your kids how to use them, too. If you think this is "yucky," just imagine what the person (a non-doggy person) who inadvertently steps in the mess thinks!

Your responsibility extends to your neighbors: To their ears (no annoying barking); to their property (their garbage, their lawn, their flower beds, their cat—especially their cat); to their kids (on bikes, at play); to their kids' toys and sports equipment.

There are numerous dog-related laws, ranging from simple dog licensing and leash laws to those holding you liable for any physical injury or property damage done by your dog. These laws are in place to protect everyone in the community, including you and your dog. There are town ordinances and state laws which are by no means the same in all towns or all states. Ignorance of the law won't get you off the hook. The time to find out what the laws are where you live is now.

Be sure your dog's license is current. This is not just a good local ordinance, it can make the difference between finding your lost dog or not.

Dressing your dog up makes him appealing to strangers.

Many states now require proof of rabies vaccination and that the dog has been spayed or neutered before issuing a license. At the same time, keep up the dog's annual immunizations.

Never let your dog run loose in the neighborhood. This will not only keep you on the right side of the leash law, it's the outdoor version of the rule about not giving your dog "freedom to get into trouble."

Good Canine Citizen

Sometimes it's hard for a dog's owner to assess whether or not the dog is sufficiently socialized to be accepted by the community at large. Does Rufus or Rufina display good, controlled behavior in public? The AKC's Canine Good Citizen program is available through many dog organizations. If your dog passes the test, the title "CGC" is earned.

The overall purpose is to turn your dog into a good neighbor and to teach you about your responsibility to your community as a dog owner. Here are the ten things your dog must do willingly:

1. Allow a stranger to handle him or her as a groomer or veterinarian would.
2. Accept a stranger stopping to chat with you.
3. Walk nicely on a loose lead.
4. Walk calmly through a crowd.
5. Sit and be petted by a stranger.
6. Sit and down on command.
7. Stay put when you move away.
8. Casually greet another dog.
9. React confidently to distractions.
10. Accept being tied up in a strange place and left alone for a few minutes.

Schools and Dogs

Schools are getting involved with pet ownership on an educational level. It has been proven that children who are kind to animals are humane in their attitude toward other people as adults.

A dog is a child's best friend, and so children are often primary pet owners, if not the primary caregivers. Unfortunately, they are also the ones most often bitten by dogs. This occurs due to a lack of understanding that pets, no matter how sweet, cuddly and loving, are still animals. Schools, along with parents, dog clubs, dog fanciers and the AKC, are working to change all that with video programs for children not only in grade school, but in the nursery school and pre-kindergarten age group. Teaching youngsters how to be responsible dog owners is important community work. When your dog has a CGC, volunteer to take part in an educational classroom event put on by your dog club.

Boy Scout Merit Badge

A Merit Badge for Dog Care can be earned by any Boy Scout ages 11 to 18. The requirements are not easy, but amount to a complete course in responsible dog care and general ownership. Here are just a few of the things a Scout must do to earn that badge:

Point out ten parts of the dog using the correct names.

Give a report (signed by parent or guardian) on your care of the dog (feeding, food used, housing, exercising, grooming and bathing), plus what has been done to keep the dog healthy.

Explain the right way to obedience train a dog, and demonstrate three comments.

Several of the requirements have to do with health care, including first aid, handling a hurt dog, and the dangers of home treatment for a serious ailment.

The final requirement is to know the local laws and ordinances involving dogs.

There are similar programs for Girl Scouts and 4-H members.

Local Clubs

Local dog clubs are no longer in existence just to put on a yearly dog show. Today, they are apt to be the hub of the community's involvement with pets. Dog clubs conduct educational forums with big-name speakers, stage demonstrations of canine talent in a busy mall and take dogs of various breeds to schools for classroom discussion.

The quickest way to feel accepted as a member in a club is to volunteer your services! Offer to help with something—anything—and watch your popularity (and your interest) grow.

Therapy Dogs

Once your dog has earned that essential CGC and reliably demonstrates a steady, calm temperament, you could look into what therapy dogs are doing in your area.

Therapy dogs go with their owners to visit patients at hospitals or nursing homes, generally remaining on leash but able to coax a pat from a stiffened hand, a smile from a blank face, a few words from sealed lips or a hug from someone in need of love.

Nursing homes cover a wide range of patient care. Some specialize in care of the elderly, some in the treatment of specific illnesses, some in physical therapy. Children's facilities also welcome visits from trained therapy dogs for boosting morale in their pediatric patients. Hospice care for the terminally ill and the at-home care of AIDS patients are other areas where this canine visiting is desperately needed. Therapy dog training comes first.

Your dog can make a difference in lots of lives.

There is a lot more involved than just taking your nice friendly pooch to someone's bedside. Doing therapy dog work involves your own emotional stability as well as that of your dog. But once you have met all the requirements for this work, making the rounds once a week or once a month with your therapy dog is possibly the most rewarding of all community activities.

Disaster Aid

This community service is definitely not for everyone, partly because it is time-consuming. The initial training is rigorous, and there can be no let-up in the continuing workouts, because members are on call 24 hours a day to go wherever they are needed at a moment's notice. But if you think you would like to be able to assist in a disaster, look into search-and-rescue work. The network of search-and-rescue volunteers is worldwide, and all members of the American Rescue Dog Association (ARDA) who are qualified to do this work are volunteers who train and maintain their own dogs.

Physical Aid

Most people are familiar with Seeing Eye dogs, which serve as blind people's eyes, but not with all the other work that dogs are trained to do to assist the disabled. Dogs are also specially trained to pull wheelchairs, carry school books, pick up dropped objects, open and close doors. Some also are ears for the deaf. All these assistance-trained dogs, by the way, are allowed anywhere "No Pet" signs exist (as are therapy dogs when properly identified). Getting started in any of this fascinating work requires a background in dog training and canine behavior, but there are also volunteer jobs ranging from answering the phone to cleaning out kennels to providing a foster home for a puppy. You have only to ask.

Making the rounds with your therapy dog can be very rewarding.

part four

Beyond
the
Basics

chapter 12

Recommended Reading

Books

ABOUT HEALTH CARE

Ackerman, Lowell. *Guide to Skin and Haircoat Problems in Dogs.* Loveland, Colo.: Alpine Publications, 1994.

Alderton, David. *The Dog Care Manual.* Hauppauge, N.Y.: Barron's Educational Series, Inc., 1986.

American Kennel Club. *American Kennel Club Dog Care and Training.* New York: Howell Book House, 1991.

Bamberger, Michelle, DVM. *Help! The Quick Guide to First Aid for Your Dog.* New York: Howell Book House, 1995.

Carlson, Delbert, DVM, and James Giffin, MD. *Dog Owner's Home Veterinary Handbook.* New York: Howell Book House, 1992.

DeBitetto, James, DVM, and Sarah Hodgson. *You & Your Puppy.* New York: Howell Book House, 1995.

Humphries, Jim, DVM. *Dr. Jim's Animal Clinic for Dogs.* New York: Howell Book House, 1994.

McGinnis, Terri. *The Well Dog Book.* New York: Random House, 1991.

Pitcairn, Richard and Susan. *Natural Health for Dogs.* Emmaus, Pa.: Rodale Press, 1982.

ABOUT DOG SHOWS

Hall, Lynn. *Dog Showing for Beginners.* New York: Howell Book House, 1994.

Nichols, Virginia Tuck. *How to Show Your Own Dog.* Neptune, N. J.: TFH, 1970.

Vanacore, Connie. *Dog Showing, An Owner's Guide.* New York: Howell Book House, 1990.

ABOUT TRAINING

Ammen, Amy. *Training in No Time*. New York: Howell Book House, 1995.

Baer, Ted. *Communicating With Your Dog*. Hauppauge, N.Y.: Barron's Educational Series, Inc., 1989.

Benjamin, Carol Lea. *Dog Problems*. New York: Howell Book House, 1989.

Benjamin, Carol Lea. *Dog Training for Kids*. New York: Howell Book House, 1988.

Benjamin, Carol Lea. *Mother Knows Best*. New York: Howell Book House, 1985.

Benjamin, Carol Lea. *Surviving Your Dog's Adolescence*. New York: Howell Book House, 1993.

Bohnenkamp, Gwen. *Manners for the Modern Dog*. San Francisco: Perfect Paws, 1990.

Dibra, Bashkim. *Dog Training by Bash*. New York: Dell, 1992.

Dunbar, Ian, PhD, MRCVS. *Dr. Dunbar's Good Little Dog Book*, James & Kenneth Publishers, 2140 Shattuck Ave. #2406, Berkeley, Calif. 94704. (510) 658–8588. Order from the publisher.

Dunbar, Ian, PhD, MRCVS. *How to Teach a New Dog Old Tricks*, James & Kenneth Publishers. Order from the publisher; address above.

Dunbar, Ian, PhD, MRCVS, and Gwen Bohnenkamp. Booklets on *Preventing Aggression; Housetraining; Chewing; Digging; Barking; Socialization; Fearfulness; and Fighting*, James & Kenneth Publishers. Order from the publisher; address above.

Evans, Job Michael. *People, Pooches and Problems*. New York: Howell Book House, 1991.

Kilcommons, Brian and Sarah Wilson. *Good Owners, Great Dogs*. New York: Warner Books, 1992.

McMains, Joel M. *Dog Logic—Companion Obedience*. New York: Howell Book House, 1992.

Rutherford, Clarice and David H. Neil, MRCVS. *How to Raise a Puppy You Can Live With*. Loveland, Colo.: Alpine Publications, 1982.

Volhard, Jack and Melissa Bartlett. *What All Good Dogs Should Know: The Sensible Way to Train*. New York: Howell Book House, 1991.

ABOUT BREEDING

Harris, Beth J. Finder. *Breeding a Litter, The Complete Book of Prenatal and Postnatal Care*. New York: Howell Book House, 1983.

Holst, Phyllis, DVM. *Canine Reproduction*. Loveland, Colo.: Alpine Publications, 1985.

Walkowicz, Chris and Bonnie Wilcox, DVM. *Successful Dog Breeding, The Complete Handbook of Canine Midwifery*. New York: Howell Book House, 1994.

ABOUT ACTIVITIES

American Rescue Dog Association. *Search and Rescue Dogs*. New York: Howell Book House, 1991.

Barwig, Susan and Stewart Hilliard. *Schutzhund*. New York: Howell Book House, 1991.

Beaman, Arthur S. *Lure Coursing*. New York: Howell Book House, 1994.

Daniels, Julie. *Enjoying Dog Agility—From Backyard to Competition*. New York: Doral Publishing, 1990.

Davis, Kathy Diamond. *Therapy Dogs*. New York: Howell Book House, 1992.

Gallup, Davis Anne. *Running With Man's Best Friend*. Loveland, Colo.: Alpine Publications, 1986.

Habgood, Dawn and Robert. *On the Road Again With Man's Best Friend*. New England, Mid-Atlantic, West Coast and Southeast editions. Selective guides to area bed and breakfasts, inns, hotels and resorts that welcome guests and their dogs. New York: Howell Book House, 1995.

Holland, Vergil S. *Herding Dogs*. New York: Howell Book House, 1994.

LaBelle, Charlene G. *Backpacking With Your Dog*. Loveland, Colo.: Alpine Publications, 1993.

Simmons-Moake, Jane. *Agility Training, The Fun Sport for All Dogs*. New York: Howell Book House, 1991.

Spencer, James B. *Hup! Training Flushing Spaniels the American Way*. New York: Howell Book House, 1992.

Spencer, James B. *Point! Training the All-Seasons Birddog*. New York: Howell Book House, 1995.

Tarrant, Bill. *Training the Hunting Retriever*. New York: Howell Book House, 1991.

Volhard, Jack and Wendy. *The Canine Good Citizen*. New York: Howell Book House, 1994.

General Titles

Haggerty, Captain Arthur J. *How to Get Your Pet Into Show Business*. New York: Howell Book House, 1994.

McLennan, Bardi. *Dogs and Kids, Parenting Tips*. New York: Howell Book House, 1993.

Moran, Patti J. *Pet Sitting for Profit, A Complete Manual for Professional Success*. New York: Howell Book House, 1992.

153

Scalisi, Danny and Libby Moses. *When Rover Just Won't Do, Over 2,000 Suggestions for Naming Your Dog.* New York: Howell Book House, 1993.

Sife, Wallace, PhD. *The Loss of a Pet.* New York: Howell Book House, 1993.

Wrede, Barbara J. *Civilizing Your Puppy.* Hauppauge, N.Y.: Barron's Educational Series, 1992.

Magazines

The AKC GAZETTE, The Official Journal for the Sport of Purebred Dogs. American Kennel Club, 51 Madison Ave., New York, NY.

Bloodlines Journal. United Kennel Club, 100 E. Kilgore Rd., Kalamazoo, MI.

Dog Fancy. Fancy Publications, 3 Burroughs, Irvine, CA 92718

Dog World. Maclean Hunter Publishing Corp., 29 N. Wacker Dr., Chicago, IL 60606.

Videos

"SIRIUS Puppy Training," by Ian Dunbar, PhD, MRCVS. James & Kenneth Publishers, 2140 Shattuck Ave. #2406, Berkeley, CA 94704. Order from the publisher.

"Training the Companion Dog," from Dr. Dunbar's British TV Series, James & Kenneth Publishers. (See address above).

The American Kennel Club produces videos on every breed of dog, as well as on hunting tests, field trials and other areas of interest to purebred dog owners. For more information, write to AKC/Video Fulfillment, 5580 Centerview Dr., Suite 200, Raleigh, NC 27606.

Resources

Breed Clubs

Every breed recognized by the American Kennel Club has a national (parent) club. National clubs are a great source of information on your breed. You can get the name of the secretary of the club by contacting:

The American Kennel Club
51 Madison Avenue
New York, NY 10010
(212) 696-8200

There are also numerous all-breed, individual breed, obedience, hunting and other special-interest dog clubs across the country. The American Kennel Club can provide you with a geographical list of clubs to find ones in your area. Contact them at the above address.

Registry Organizations

Registry organizations register purebred dogs. The American Kennel Club is the oldest and largest in this country, and currently recognizes over 130 breeds. The United Kennel Club registers some breeds the AKC doesn't (including the American Pit Bull Terrier and the Miniature Fox Terrier) as well as many of the same breeds. The others included here are for your reference; the AKC can provide you with a list of foreign registries.

American Kennel Club
51 Madison Avenue
New York, NY 10010

United Kennel Club (UKC)
100 E. Kilgore Road
Kalamazoo, MI 49001-5598

American Dog Breeders Assn.
P.O. Box 1771
Salt Lake City, UT 84110
(Registers American Pit Bull Terriers)

Canadian Kennel Club
89 Skyway Avenue
Etobicoke, Ontario
Canada M9W 6R4

National Stock Dog Registry
P.O. Box 402
Butler, IN 46721
(Registers working stock dogs)

Orthopedic Foundation for Animals (OFA)
2300 E. Nifong Blvd.
Columbia, MO 65201-3856
(Hip registry)

Activity Clubs

Write to these organizations for information on the
activities they sponsor.

American Kennel Club
51 Madison Avenue
New York, NY 10010
(Conformation Shows, Obedience Trials, Field
Trials and Hunting Tests, Agility, Canine Good

Citizen, Lure Coursing, Herding, Tracking, Earthdog Tests, Coonhunting.)

United Kennel Club
100 E. Kilgore Road
Kalamazoo, MI 49001-5598
(Conformation Shows, Obedience Trials, Agility, Hunting for Various Breeds, Terrier Trials and more.)

North American Flyball Assn.
1342 Jeff St.
Ypsilanti, MI 48198

International Sled Dog Racing Assn.
P.O. Box 446
Norman, ID 83848-0446

North American Working Dog Assn., Inc.
Southeast Kreisgruppe
P.O. Box 833
Brunswick, GA 31521

Trainers

Association of Pet Dog Trainers
P.O. Box 3734
Salinas, CA 93912
(408) 663–9257

American Dog Trainers' Network
161 West 4th St.
New York, NY 10014
(212) 727–7257

National Association of Dog Obedience Instructors
2286 East Steel Rd.
St. Johns, MI 48879

Associations

American Dog Owners Assn.
1654 Columbia Tpk.
Castleton, NY 12033
(Combats anti-dog legislation)

Delta Society
P.O. Box 1080
Renton, WA 98057-1080
(Promotes the human/animal bond through
pet-assisted therapy and other programs)

Dog Writers Assn. of America (DWAA)
Sally Cooper, Secy.
222 Woodchuck Ln.
Harwinton, CT 06791

National Assn. for Search and Rescue (NASAR)
P.O. Box 3709
Fairfax, VA 22038

Therapy Dogs International
1536 Morris Place
Hillside, NJ 07205